Book #1

Bursting from Extinction to Distinction

Created by Heather Rancourt
Written by Heather Rancourt and Claudia Gauches

Published by 360 Marketing LLC
Stonington, CT 06378

The Fossibles: *Bursting from Extinction to Distinction*

ISBN 978-0-9702654-5-6

Second Edition
Printed in the USA

This book is dedicated to all the children
throughout the world who believe
anything's fossible!

www.thefossibles.com

Listen to what other Fossi Fans have to say.

From the first person to read the book, Hugo, Age 7

"I love the Fossibles. ... I know it is going to be a great book
and a great movie. I just love it. BRAVO, BRAVO!!!!

"I liked reading the book and can't wait to read the next one."

Parker, Age 10

"I read the Fossibles! It's a great book to read. My little
brother and sister really want my mom to read this book to
them. They can not wait to buy it."

Emily, Age 7

"Thank you for writing such a great book. Parker and Charlie
got home and immediately went to the Fossibles website.
They were blown away! ... We are ALL looking forward to
the next book."

The Murray Family

www.thefossibles.com

ACKNOWLEDGEMENT
FROM THE CREATOR OF THE FOSSIBLES,
HEATHER RANCOURT

To my husband Sean, thank you for your constant love and support, infinity! Thank you to my son, Chase, for giving me inspiration and my son, Camden, for giving me even more inspiration. Joan and Clem, thank you for all your love and support. To my best friend and brother, Brent, thank you and I think we call this a "good one!" Dad, I appreciate all your encouragement and support. Finally to the co-author, who also happens to be my mother, without you none of this would have been Fossible! I love you and thank you!

www.thefossibles.com

www.thefossibles.com

Table of Contents

www.thefossibles.com

CHAPTER 1

A Long, Long Time Ago

Sheets of rain pour down along the coastline of a great landmass that will, in about sixty-five million years, be known as the United States of America. Darkness overtakes this primitive land as a steady, unforgiving rain pelts down on heavy vegetation that looks like an army of mysterious, dark, threatening creatures bending in the wind on this, the very deepest of nights.

Huddled at the entrance to a cave, two tyrannosaurs nudge each other and utter loud, scary noises. Off in the distance, other dinosaur species trudge slowly up the hill toward the cave. Their huge feet slop loudly in the rainwater puddling on the earth as a result of this humongous downpour. As the approaching dinosaurs come slowly into view near the entrance to the cave, they mutter to themselves.

Despite the "survival of the fittest" pecking order that is natural among the dinosaurs, on this night, the stronger species do not attack the weaker ones. For tonight is indeed a very special night. All the dinosaurs are on a most important mission. There is something each of them must do before daybreak.

Earlier in the day, word spread quickly among all the dinosaurs of the land. Two representatives of each dinosaur species were instructed to appear at the entrance to this cave once night fell. Summoned by the reigning Dinosaur Magistrate, Zigopholus, each was told to bring along at least one dinosaur egg from their species.

Now, at this late hour, Zigopholus himself stands at the entrance to the cave and greets each arriving dinosaur duo. He clutches a crooked wooden staff with a big red crystal on top that is always by his side to help him navigate across the vast terrain of the Crystal Red Supremacy that he oversees.

Graciously, Zigopholus motions the arriving dinosaurs into the cave where it is warm, dry, and well-lit by numerous robust fires burning along the rocky walls. Highly respectful of Zigopholus, each dinosaur enters the cave only when directed by him to do so. The bright red orange fires take over where the heavy rain leaves off, casting enormous, frightful images onto the walls of the cave. Firelight eerily flickers in the eyes of each of the massive creatures gathered here tonight and is distracting to all. They look nervously from one to the other. Stalagmites coming up from the floor and stalactites hanging down from the ceiling make it difficult for some of the more bulky dinosaurs to get comfortable.

Once all are gathered in the cave, Zigopholus steps inside and greets the dinosaurs warmly. "Thank you all for responding to my urgent call earlier today. I have something very important to tell you and I want you to carry my message back to all other dinosaurs among your species. As you know, within the office of the Crystal Red Supremacy that I control, we are always on the look-out for anything that could jeopardize our lives here on this planet. Today, I am sad to tell you that we have intercepted intelligence from another planet, Osteroya, leading us to believe that all of our lives are in immediate danger. We are certain that the Royans who live on Osteroya are intent on permanently eliminating all dinosaurs from this land so that they can take it over for themselves. Trust me. We will do our best to fight back, but ..."

"But how, sir? How will we fight off the Royans?" bellows Brauntis One, the most powerful brontosaurus of the land.

"Hear me out, Brauntis One," responds Zigopholus. "Let me explain."

Speaking slowly and with a voice filled with emotion, Zigopholus continues. "In truth, we may not be able to save ourselves, but we can insure that, at some point many years from now, dinosaurs will once again live and thrive on this planet. That's why I asked each of you to bring one or more dinosaur eggs from your species with you tonight. With help from all who are gathered here in this cave, we will bury each egg deep beneath the surface, so deep that the eggs may not be found for millions and millions of years. But, when they are found ..."

Suddenly, a triceratops named Jiriz, interrupts angrily. "What do you mean we may not be able to save ourselves? I've got a lot of great things going on in my life and don't want to think about..."

"Stop," orders Zigopholus forcefully. "Stop right now. I'll hear none of that."

"Jiriz, be quiet for once and listen. Tonight it's very important that we all listen carefully to the Magistrate," says an impatient parasaurolophus named Spedeb.

Zigopholus continues. "Our mission tonight is not to talk about things we cannot change. Rather, it is to take action so that future creatures on this planet will someday learn the truth about dinosaurs. Years from now when the dinosaur eggs that we are about to bury are discovered, hopefully some will hatch. Then, the world that welcomes the new, young dinosaurs will learn just how powerful we were. They'll know that, if dinosaurs could survive and flourish over such a vast expanse of time, anything's possible. Thus, each of us gathered here tonight will be bonded together forever by the mission we are about to perform. After all, it is we who are creating a very special dinosaur legacy for all who follow us onto this planet."

Tears glisten in the corner of his eyes, yet he pushes on. "Now, let's get started. I fear we don't have very much time. Come on. Some of you big guys, get over here and let's start digging. Please line up behind me with your eggs. I will say a blessing over each egg before we bury it."

Two tyrannosaurs, Rex and Tytrex, move clumsily to the area where the eggs will be buried. Not good at digging, they enlist the help of other dinosaurs with better arm strength and use some primitive tools stocked in the cave. Dirt flies as holes are dug deep into the ground. They create separate pockets for each of the bowling ball sized eggs. The burning fires provide light. Rain continues to pour down outside and cascades in a loud, heavy, gray sheet at the entrance to the cave.

One by one, each dinosaur pair approaches Zigopholus and hands over the eggs from their dinosaur species. Carefully, Zigopholus accepts each egg and passes his special staff with the red crystal on top over it. In turn, he says to each dinosaur, "Tonight, you have done a great service for dinosaurs. As Magistrate, I officially recognize you as a bona fide participant in our attempt to ward off the evil of Osteroya and to save your species. May you continue to operate with strong values throughout the remainder of your life. Good night, my friend. And, thank you." When his words are complete, Zigopholus removes a smooth, cool stone from the pocket of an enormous purple shawl thrown about his neck and slips it into each dinosaur's hand for one last measure of good luck.

With their mission complete, each dinosaur trudges out of the cave and into a rainy day that is dawning after a very long, dark night. Unsure of what their own futures hold based on the impending threat from Osteroya, each finds comfort knowing that they have buried at least one of their eggs deep within the cavern. Running off toward their homes, rain continues to engulf them. The sound of large, slushing footsteps fills the wet air.

After all the dinosaurs leave the cave, Zigopholus raises his prized staff to his lips and secretly whispers into the glistening red crystal on top of it. Then, he gently lays the staff across a sizable patch of earth covering numerous newly-buried eggs. Huge tears run freely down his face and splash loudly to earth, creating instant puddles in the fresh-turned soil on which he stands.

Slowly, he turns and lumbers to the entrance of the cave. Looking back one last time, Zigopholus knows that the future of all dinosaurs is indeed unknown. Suspecting that there isn't much time left, he turns and runs from the cave. His purple shawl unravels from around his neck and flaps wildly about his face. His huge feet stick in the deep, fresh mud and it takes lots of energy to extract each footstep and continue to run. His tremendous weight causes boulders to scatter onto the path in front of him as he heads for home.

For all the dinosaurs of the Crystal Red Supremacy, including Zigopholus, the day that has just dawned has brought with it the worse kind of uncertainty. Who really knows what lies ahead?

www.thefossibles.com

CHAPTER 2

Scrambled Eggs

And so, in the mere blink of an eye in terms of the nearly two billion years our planet has existed, all dinosaurs vanished. They simply vanished.

Zigopholus spoke the truth on that night sixty-five million years ago when he gathered all the dinosaur species into a cave somewhere along the rocky coast of the continent and warned them of a very real, impending threat.

To this day, no one is really sure what actually happened to the dinosaurs or how they became extinct. Were the Royans successful? We may never know the answer to that question. But, one thing's for sure. The dinosaurs disappeared. That is, all except those unborn dinosaurs nestled snuggly in eggs buried deep beneath the surface of the earth in that very special cave.

For millions and millions of years after the eggs were buried, not much happened. That is, not until about fifteen to twenty million years ago.

Then, the crust of the earth began to violently rip apart in various places. Huge chunks of rock crashed down forming new jagged mountains and carving flatter, more serene valleys. The coastline filled in and moved farther west. The cave that had been on the coastline when the dinosaurs gathered there millions of years ago, was now situated to the east in a hot, desert area.

Violent eruptions repeatedly shook the earth to its very core. Some of the buried eggs did not withstand the sharp movements in the earth. Their shells, although tougher than most eggs, shattered and spilled their slippery contents out onto the dry dirt that had encased them. Quickly, the embryos moistened the very earth that had sheltered them for millions of years. And, just as quickly, the dry, hungry earth absorbed them. And so, they too simply disappeared.

Loud crashing noises accompanied by dramatic earth changes persisted. Over time, more and more of the hidden dinosaur eggs cracked and their contents were destroyed.

But some of the eggs survived the ordeal of earth's ferocious dance. As the earth shifted, many lost the safety and shelter of being completely buried deep in the dirt. Gradually, various parts of the eggs became exposed. Miraculously, the cave itself stayed in tact. It remained exactly as it had been the night Zigopholus gathered all the dinosaurs together within the safety of its walls millions and millions of years before.

CHAPTER 3

Go West, Young Man, Go West!

In a college in the Northeast, a mild-mannered professor named Clem Stone is lecturing to a class of about one hundred students seated in front of him in a stadium-style classroom. The students' attention ranges from some who are sitting on the edge of their seats taking notes to several who aren't listening to him at all.

One boy has his head pitched back against his seat and is sleeping soundly with his mouth wide open. This kid hasn't begun to snore yet, but Clem knows that, any minute now, he will. It always happens this way. A loud, ferocious snore cuts into the rhythm of his lecture. Inevitably, the dreaded snore abruptly wakes the kid who let it rip, followed immediately by the entire classroom erupting into laughter. Prepared, Clem braces for the boy's snore.

It's late in the afternoon on a crisp, cool day in early November. Cold and rainy, leaves are falling against the many small window panes along the back wall of the lecture hall reminding Clem that winter will soon be here. And, winter in the Northeast means lots and lots of snow.

Clem is a professor of Information Technology, his specialty. Today, he's explaining a newer version of computers to the students. He's talking about networking computers in a virtual environment.

He's been teaching at this college for a couple of years and, quite frankly, he's tired of it. So is his wife, Joan. Neither one likes the long, dark, cold New England winters. Last year, they vacationed in Arizona during semester break in December and, ever since then, have longed to just pack it in and move there.

Today, Clem finds himself daydreaming throughout his lecture. Looking out across the classroom, he sees some disinterested kids, a very dreary day, and, in the reflection of the computer screen in front of him, he sees his own image. He looks tired.

Clem is ready for a change. He's always dreamed of leaving the teaching profession and opening a motorcycle repair shop. Motorcycles are his very favorite thing in life. That is, after his wife, Joan. And Clem loves to invent things, everything from household items to gadgets that utilize the technology he knows so much about.

His hi-tech inventions are amazing. He's invented gadgets that no one else has even thought about. Right now, he's got over one hundred and fifty patents pending with the U.S. Patent and Trademark Office in Washington, D.C.

A really funny thing about Clem, though, is that he has difficulty repairing everyday household gadgets. In fact, Joan tells the story of the time Clem tried to repair their radio. He took it all apart and laid out all the inner workings on an old newspaper spread out on top of the kitchen table. Once he was convinced he had fixed it, he meticulously reassembled the radio. The only problem was, he had a couple of extra parts left over. So, he just threw them away, hoping Joan wouldn't notice. When the repaired radio was first plugged in, it seemed to work fine. That is, until Joan tried to turn it off. It wouldn't turn off when she pressed the "off" button. But, as soon as she walked away from it, the radio magically turned off. It was almost as if the radio was self-conscious and didn't want to turn off when anyone was close by or looking at it. Over time, the radio took on a life of its own. Soon, it became impossible to turn the radio on with the "on" button too. Either Joan or Clem had to push the "on" or "off" button and then walk away. Then and only then would the radio do what they wanted it to do. A very strange radio indeed! Bashful and defiant!

On this cold November day, Clem continues to daydream about moving to Arizona as he lectures to his students. He survives the loud snore when it comes, a snore that causes the young man who emits it to fall out of his chair.

Later that night when he's home with Joan, Clem waits for the right time and finally says, "Joan, I was thinking today about Arizona. Both of us really enjoyed it so much when we were there last winter. What would you think about moving to Arizona before the end of the year? I'd love to open a motorcycle repair shop. It's been my life dream. And you like to exercise and walk every day. Imagine how great it would be if snow storms didn't cut into your outdoor walks? What do you say? We don't have any kids. There's nothing holding us here. There's no reason we should stay here for another long, cold winter."

Joan stares at him from across the room, remaining silent. Clem rumples the newspaper he's reading and fidgets in his big overstuffed easy chair, unsure of what to expect.

Finally, Joan speaks. "I say, it's OK with me. I've been thinking about it myself but was afraid to bring up the subject. Looks like you beat me to it. When can we leave?"

"Whoa! Whoa! You're moving too fast. We don't even have a place to live yet. We'll need a place to call home," Clem says displaying slight hesitation for the first time.

"Why do we need to have a place to live before we get there, Clem? Let's just go out to Arizona and drive around until we find a place we both like. That way, we won't rush into making a quick decision. What do you say? If you're game, I'm game."

"OK, honey, you've got a deal. I'll tender my resignation tomorrow, effective at the end of this semester."

"I can't believe it. I thought you'd never give up teaching."

"I know," Clem continues. "But when you agreed so quickly to a motorcycle repair shop, that's all I needed to hear. Good-bye, college classroom. Hello, to that new bright yellow motorcycle I've had my eyes on for a couple of years. Arizona is looking better and better."

"Hold on, Clem. I might want to get into something new myself once we get there."

"That's OK with me. I know you like to keep busy. I'm sure you'll find something to do."

"I always do."

"I know. But doesn't this seem like the right thing for us to do. Doesn't it? Somehow, and I don't know why, I get a funny feeling that Arizona is calling to us."

"Are you sure it isn't that new yellow motorcycle that's calling to you?" Joan asks, laughing.

Their conversation ends as each scurries off to a different part of the house to write a "To Do" list for their impending move.

www.thefossibles.com

CHAPTER 4

Red Rocks Rock

At the end of the year, Clem and Joan moved to their new home at the base of the red rock mountains on the outskirts of Phoenix, Arizona. The home they selected was typical for the area-stucco construction with a tile roof. The great thing about the home they bought was that it came with a lot of land, about seventy-five acres.

The land itself was hilly and rocky in places. In other places, it was flat and covered with dry, parched earth. Beautiful red rocks either popped out of the flat surface of the land or tumbled down on top of each other like a game of marbles played by giants. Cactus poked out of the red dirt all over the property. Although many different varieties flourished, it was mainly the saguaro cactus that punctuated their new land. These cacti looked like soldiers standing guard, prickly creatures with two long arms pointed skyward.

Their new house was perfect for Joan and Clem. It was just the right size. They had no children, so three bedrooms were more than enough. Joan quickly turned one of the extra bedrooms into a sewing room and Clem converted the other into a TV room, big screen TV and all.

One of the things Clem liked most about their new house was the workshop/garage attached to it. The former owner had repaired home appliances, including washing machines, in the workshop. Now, it was perfect for Clem's motorcycle repair business.

Soon, Clem's motorcycle shop opened for business. On the first day of business, he walked down the dusty, long driveway to the main road and ceremoniously tacked up a sign with a big arrow pointing up to the house. The sign read simply, "Clem's Motorcycle Repairs" with the phone number beneath it. Clem felt very proud when he hung the sign for all passers-by to see.

And there were lots of passers-by on the road at the end of the Stones' driveway. Motorcycles went by all day long. Because there wasn't another repair shop within twenty-five miles, before long, Clem had a waiting list of people intent on having him, and him alone, fix their treasured bike. Whenever anyone spoke with Clem, it was immediately apparent that he knew more than most about motorcycles. Consequently, his reputation spread quickly throughout Arizona and the surrounding states.

Joan got her daily exercise by exploring the seventy-five acres they now owned. She'd take off at sunrise carrying a walking stick and wearing new hiking boots she'd bought in Phoenix. Always particular about her clothes, she made herself several pairs of new walking shorts to help her keep cool in the stifling Arizona heat. A fanny pack was always attached at her waist. In it, she carried sunscreen, first aid items, and a little bit of money. Picking up a bottle of water from the fridge and putting on her prescription sunglasses so that she wouldn't miss anything, she'd take off on long walks, so curious about every nook and cranny of their new property. Some days, when he wasn't really busy, Clem joined her.

If Clem went along, he had his own ideas about what he needed to bring. First, he definitely needed more than SPF 45 sunscreen to protect his bald head from the unforgiving Arizona sun, so he usually brought along a wide-brimmed hat. Although his work belt was normally filled with an array of tools that he used while repairing motorcycles, on days he walked with Joan, it was loaded with other items, such as a flashlight, lantern, map, compass, cell phone, dry food, water, and more. That way, if he and Joan got lost or hurt, at least they'd have the tools they needed to survive and get help. Also, Clem bought himself a pair of the best walking shoes made so that his feet would be comfortable whenever he accompanied Joan on a walk.

One day, Joan and Clem walked to the farthest northwestern corner of their property. It was rocky and mountainous. Some of the slopes they climbed were so steep that both of them lost their breath. One particular rock mountain really intrigued Joan from afar as the two approached. She decided that she and Clem should climb to the top of it. And so, when they got to its base, they started up the side of the mountain.

When they were midway up, the sky suddenly turned dark and threatening. It looked like it would open up at any minute and drench them with a severe rainstorm. Both were frightened because a strong rain could easily wash away the fragile path they were walking on and possibly cause a rockslide as well.

"We better look for a place to get out of this storm. I don't think we have long before it will be pouring buckets," Clem barked as a strong wind began to whip up.

"I know. I know. But where can we go. Do you see any place to take cover?" Joan responded nervously.

Both stopped for a moment and looked up and down the mountain they were on. At first, neither saw anything that looked promising. But then Clem noticed a big, black, jagged square on the side of a humongous rock on one of the highest points on the mountain. It looked like a huge, dark door to a giant's house. But, Clem suspected it was more than just a black-colored rock. He sensed that it was actually a large opening, perhaps an opening to a cave.

"Look, Joan. Look over there," he said as he pointed toward the dark colored rock. "I think it's a cave. Can it be?"

"It sure looks like a cave. Let's go."

Clem and Joan walked at a fast pace toward the black colored square on the side of the mountain. As they got closer, they knew it was a cave because they could clearly see the opening. When they were about one hundred yards from it, the heavens opened up and strong rain pelted them, hurting their skin. It was difficult to see as sheets of heavy, silver rain pounded down. Clem grabbed Joan's hand and together they ran toward the cave.

Finally, they bounded through the cave entrance escaping the downpour. Joan shook her hair to get the excess rain out. Clem took his hat off and wrung it out. Then, he wiped his bald head with a handkerchief he pulled from the pocket of his pants. Both took a moment to catch their breath. Suddenly, the sheer darkness of the cave began to frighten them. Each wondered silently what lurked inside.

Clem flicked on a flashlight. All they could see were huge rock walls inside the cave. He handed the flashlight to Joan. Then, he lit his lantern for more light. Bravely, he held the lantern with one hand and took Joan's hand with his other. Together, they began to cautiously walk farther back to explore the cave.

The inside of the cave was very eerie. It felt as if spirits from the past were gathered here, hovering around them as they walked. Joan especially felt like an intruder in a place she hadn't been invited. She became very scared and started to shake. Clem, although he didn't say it, sensed the same thing — unknown spirits lurking nearby.

The walls of the cave were colored black as if strong fires had once raged up their surfaces. The floor of the cave was uneven and littered with boulders, some the size of a car. Hearing the rain still pouring down outside, Clem and Joan ignored their fears and continued to walk farther back into the cave. Soon, they came upon what appeared to be a separate room within the cave. Peering inside, both stopped dead in their tracks.

The room contained a lot of huge rocks thrown on top of each other, perhaps from all the changes in the earth over time. Yet, in the middle of the room, four odd vertical rock formations protruded from the floor of the cave. Perched on top of each rock was a huge, bowling ball sized egg. A couple of the eggs were about to fall off the rock pillar that supported them and crash violently onto the cave floor.

"What are those? Are those eggs? Look at the size of them!" exclaimed Joan.

"I have no idea. Whatever is in those eggs, it must be mighty big. I've never seen an egg that size. Maybe we should get out of here. I don't want to meet the creature that laid those eggs. Let's get going."

"No, no, we can't just leave them here. Look at those two on the end. They're about to fall. Let's take them home with us. Aren't you interested in finding out what's inside these eggs?" asked Joan.

"Right now, I'm more worried about who the heck left them here. I'm getting a really weird feeling in this cave. If you want to take them home, let's get moving. Rain or no rain, we're getting out of here as soon as we can," Clem stated firmly.

Quickly, yet with care, Joan and Clem lifted each egg off its perch and walked it back to the cave entrance. By the time they had moved all four eggs to the cave entrance, the rainstorm had passed. The sun was starting to peak through. It was still morning, so the desert temperature remained bearable.

"What should we do now?" Joan asked.

"Do you want to wait here while I go back and get my truck and a wheelbarrow so we can get these eggs out of here and down the mountain without breaking them?" he asked.

When Joan didn't respond, he continued, "Joan, what's the matter? Are you afraid to wait here by yourself?"

"Yes, I'm afraid. I don't want to meet up with whatever left these eggs either."

"You have your cell phone with you, don't you?"

"Yes, but what good is that? I'm afraid of this cave, Clem. It's spooky."

"OK, OK. Let's take our chances then. Leave the eggs right here and we'll both go back home for the truck and other stuff we need."

"Thanks. That makes me feel a lot better. Let's hurry."

CHAPTER 5

Surprise! Surprise!

By late that same day, Joan and Clem had safely brought all four huge eggs back to their home. None of the eggs were damaged as they traveled in the bed of Clem's truck that was lined with a big, soft, puffy comforter taken from their bed. Joan rode in the back of the truck to help insure the eggs didn't crash into each other and break.

When they got to their house, Joan went into the kitchen and got four huge bowls out of the cupboard. She lined each bowl with a large bath towel and placed an egg in each one. Then, she placed the bowls on her plant shelf under the plant lamps she used to cultivate her African violets. The plant shelf was off to one side in the kitchen. It wasn't a place that Joan and Clem noticed very much. Plants just sort of sat quietly on the shelf and flourished under Joan's care. That is until now. These eggs weren't content to just sit there and keep quiet.

One morning at about 4:30 a.m., Joan and Clem heard a loud cracking sound coming from the kitchen as they slept in their bedroom down the hall.

"What's that noise, Clem? It sounds like someone's in the kitchen."

"I don't know. Let me go check," he said, getting out of bed and pulling on his jeans.

Joan heard Clem walk carefully down the hall, unsure of what he'd find once he got to the kitchen. Suddenly, she heard another loud cracking sound, louder than the first.

"Clem, what is it? Are you alright?" she yelled.

"Honey, come here. You're not going to believe this!" Clem replied excitedly.

Joan grabbed her robe and ran into the kitchen. At first, she didn't see anything other than Clem grinning at her, eyes wide with amazement. Then, she heard a third loud cracking sound. It came from the plant shelf. She turned toward the shelf. As she did so, a fourth cracking sound pierced the early morning silence.

"Oh my, Clem, the eggs have hatched. What the heck are those things?" Joan asked while closely surveying the four lizard-like heads dizzily popping through the thick, cracked eggshells.

Clem moved closer too. "If I didn't know any better, I'd say they're dinosaurs."

"Dinosaurs! Dinosaurs! How can that be? Dinosaurs haven't lived on this planet for millions and millions of years!"

"You've got me. But, I think we've discovered something that will interest every scientist on the planet. We could become rich and famous on this one. Let me check them out on the Internet."

Clem went to his computer and quickly returned with drawings and information on each dinosaur species. He determined that they had just witnessed the birth of one tyrannosaur, one parasaurolophus, one brontosaurus, and one triceratops.

Upon further examination, he also determined that they had two boys, the tyrannosaur and the brontosaurus, and two girls, the triceratops and the parasaurolophus.

"Clem, they're so cute. Let's keep them here and not tell anyone. We can raise them as our own, the children we never had. If we let the world know about them, they'll be taken from us. They won't have any freedom or any real future. They'll be held captive by scientists from around the world who will analyze everything about them. Let's give them a chance to just be kids, our kids. What do you say?"

Clem thought about it for a long time. He made some coffee, waited for it to perk and still didn't respond. Finally, he said, "OK, honey. I have my motorcycle shop, why shouldn't you have something that you really enjoy too. I know you've always wanted children. So, I say, it's OK with me. We'll just have to make sure that none of my customers or our friends see them. Is that going to be difficult? Can we keep them a secret?

"I think we can, especially while they're still so young."

"Then we've got a deal. Now, let's do what all new parents do. Let's give them names."

Joan looked at Clem, unsure of what she wanted to name them. Clem, who usually was silent about things like this, spoke right away. It was as if he was getting a message piped into his brain from another time and place, some type of force that knew all about dinosaurs, especially these dinosaurs, and had very strong ideas on what their names should be.

"Let's name one boy, the tyrannosaur, Trex. The other boy, the brontosaurus, let's call him simply Braun. The girls are a different story. How about Deb for the parasaurolophus and Riz for the triceratops? Do you like the sounds of those names?"

"Yes, I sure do," Joan responded, unsure of where or how Clem had come up with names so quickly. He normally was far more contemplative and slow to make a decision. It seemed like a special force was driving him. "Now, let me get started on being a mother. I have to clean them up, make sure they're warm, and give them each some milk. Meantime, you must head off to the store in Phoenix to buy cribs and all the other things they'll need. I'll make a list. And while you're at it, Clem, you'd better empty out your TV room. It's now a nursery."

"OK, Mom. I hear you."

www.thefossibles.com

CHAPTER 6

He's Not Digging This

Dr. Dimitri Roy, a world famous paleontologist, is supervising a dinosaur dig in eastern Montana. Attempting to discover, identify, and excavate dinosaur remains has been Dr. Roy's life work for many years. He travels throughout the world in search of a remarkable dinosaur discovery that will instantly immortalize him among the ranks of all paleontologists and bring him the fame and fortune he so desperately seeks.

On this particular dig, he's growing increasingly frustrated because it has not been successful yet. Nothing of consequence has been unearthed. The weather is hot and sticky. Loose dirt continuously swirls through the air. Despite the heat, Dr. Roy wears the clothes he always wears-a dark vest, white button shirt, ascot, dungaree pants, and knee-high boots. His sidekick, a black crow, is usually perched on his shoulder and only flies away when Dr. Roy relentlessly swats at him.

The more frustrated Dr. Roy gets, the more he yells at the people doing the actual work. Some are paid staff while others are volunteers. Each and every one of them has a strong interest in dinosaurs. They think Dr. Roy is strange when he rants and raves. Often walking in circles and mumbling to himself under his breath, Dr. Roy occasionally throws one of the dig tools out of the dig site for emphasis. Then, he storms off and retreats to the tent he shares with his bird.

All of the people working on the dig are camping at the site rather than commuting daily to and from the nearest town. The tents they live in are not luxurious, but they are adequate, particularly Dr. Roy's tent. As the leader of the dig, he gets a tent all to himself. That is, he and his bird have a tent all to themselves.

Despite the air of organization and precision that Dr. Roy likes to convey to others, in reality, he's obsessed by an odd fear for a man of his age. He's very afraid of the dark. Consequently, this dig has taken a toll on him. Each night, unable to sleep, he lays in the darkness of his tent and listens to the night noises rolling across the Montana landscape. If his bird makes any sound at all, he slaps at him to be quiet so that he can tell exactly where the outside noises are coming from. Afraid to shut his eyes, he lays in bed with his eyes wide open. This has been going on night after night as he stands guard against the incredible darkness surrounding his tent.

Lack of sleep does strange things to people. And, Dr. Roy is no exception. Over time, he's become very irritable. His incoherent mumbling has increased. His heavy eyelids droop down over his eyes making them appear shut. He trembles a bit, particularly his hands when he's trying to write.

Then, one morning about 4:30 a.m., Dr. Roy begins to have uncontrollable tremors throughout his body. Lying in bed, his arms and legs shake relentlessly as if an earthquake is inside of him. His head flops frantically from side to side. He lets out a blood curdling roar, similar to one of an actual dinosaur. Suddenly the seizure stops. Dr. Roy, unsure of what has just happened, sighs with relief and relaxes his body once again into the cot on which he sleeps.

But, in about five minutes, the same thing happens again. And, again five minutes later. And, finally, for a fourth time, five minutes after that. During the quiet intervals between seizures, Dr. Roy lays still with his eyes wide open, afraid to move. His bird stays by his side with a puzzled expression on his face.

Finally, Dr. Roy swats angrily at him.

"Shhhhhhhhooooooo! Get away from me! Go! Leave me alone!"

The bird flies up to the top of the tent, but doesn't fly out as Dr. Roy has told it to. Instead, the bird hovers above, unsure of what is happening to his buddy. These four unexplainable seizures are troubling, not only for Dr. Roy, but for his loyal bird.

None too soon, the early morning sun rises in the east and the darkness of night begins to evaporate.

After this most eventful sleepless night, Dr. Roy now faces an exhaustive day at the dig. But today, unlike other days when it was a chore for him to get his tired body out of bed, Dr. Roy eagerly jumps off his cot, dresses, and bolts from his tent. Unsure of what the four seizures he just had were all about, he's eager to put his mind in another place and dig into the dig.

CHAPTER 7

Groooowing Up!

As the four dinosaurs grew, so too did their unique personalities. Each formed their own likes, dislikes, strengths, and weakness. Individually, they began to explore the world around them and each viewed what they saw from their own perspective.

From infancy, Joan taught each dinosaur how to speak English. Deb and Trex became more proficient at it earlier than Riz and Braun did. When Deb was four years old, Joan noticed that she had the ability to speak and understand other languages very easily. As she got older, she continued to develop this skill and learn more languages. By the time she was eight, Deb spoke fluent Italian, Spanish, Chinese, and Russian. She continually amazed the entire family with her special language talent.

Braun, on the other hand, was known for interjecting lots of cool expressions into his speech that he picked up from television. Utterances, like "Boo-Yah," "Dude," and others flowed off his tongue. Eventually, he simply created his own slang. For example, whenever anyone in the family did something Braun approved of (like passing one of Joan's math tests), he signified his approval by looking directly into the eyes of the person he wanted to congratulate and drawling BONE-A-FIDE in a very deep voice. Quickly, BONE-A-FIDE became his very favorite expression and he said it many, many times throughout the day, a fact that drove Deb crazy.

"Mom, it is so hard to concentrate on schoolwork with him constantly saying BONE-A-FIDE. Plus, it doesn't even make any sense," Deb stammered.

"Oh, it doesn't make any sense, Deb? Well, it makes more sense than listening to you talk Russian and not understanding one word you say," growled Braun. "You think you're so smart. In case you haven't noticed, we speak English in this house. And, "bona fide" is an English word. I've just changed it a little to reflect the fact that we're dinosaurs and to honor our ancestors, many of whom are, unfortunately, just nameless bones assembled in museums. That's why I spell it B-O-N-E-A..."

"It may very well be an English word ..." Deb began to interrupt Braun, but Joan cut her off.

"Now, now, stop fighting. We've listened to the two of you bicker more than any of us care to. Braun, go outside for a while and leave Deb alone. Deb, clean up your computer desk so Trex can use it later," ordered Joan. "Let's all meet back here in ten minutes."

All four dinosaurs dispersed quickly. Riz went to the refrigerator for a bottle of Dino-Ade and Trex jumped on the treadmill to pass the time. Deb went to her room and Braun went outside.

That's how life was for the four dinosaurs and their parents. Joan home-schooled them and split the group up or called a break whenever they weren't getting along. That way, everyone had time to cool off and come to their senses. Joan was determined not to let rifts between the four dinosaurs take control of her home or her schooling agenda. Joan and Clem worked very hard at making sure that all four of their dinosaur children respected and protected each other.

In home school, the dinosaurs learned subjects like English, math, history, science, and geography. Joan also taught them all about their dinosaur ancestors and what the earth was like in prehistoric times. Most important, Joan and Clem taught their kids strong personal values—honesty, integrity, trust, acceptance, helping others, kindness, and so much more.

From the beginning, Joan and Clem explained to the dinosaurs that they were different from human kids. They instructed them not to allow themselves to be seen by humans because, if they were to be seen, they might be in grave danger. After all, people all over the world believed that dinosaurs were extinct. If their existence became known, everyone would want a piece of them, especially scientists who would examine them, analyze their DNA, control their environment, poke and prod, and, worst of all, treat them like dinosaurs instead of the human-like kids they'd become.

So the dinosaurs relied on the Internet and chat rooms to make contact with human kids. Cyber space became their primary communication tool. Each could talk to as many kids as they wanted and not one of the human kids realized they were actually talking to a live dinosaur living a pretty cool life somewhere in Arizona.

When the dinosaurs weren't studying, they watched TV, exercised, surfed the Net, or rough-housed with each other. However, because rough-housing caused major damage to the interior of the Stones' home, the dinosaurs were instructed to go outside if they wanted to play like that.

Trex and Braun were often found hanging around Clem's motorcycle repair shop and learning how mechanical things work. Lots of times, the two of them lifted weights in a makeshift gym Clem constructed for them on the side of the house.

Braun developed a real fondness for all kinds of music, especially island music. He'd play CDs in the living room and dance. Slow, cumbersome, and intent on moving to the music, he'd dance for hours on end. On days when he played fast music, his huge, unwieldy tail whipped around uncontrollably and knocked everything off the coffee table in front of the TV. Regardless, Braun kept dancing.

Riz was always preparing for the future she envisioned for herself. She wanted to be the first dinosaur with a TV talk show. Consequently, she always rehearsed in preparation for the day she'd be "discovered" and her dream would become a reality. From the living room, Braun, and Trex could hear Riz introducing herself to an imaginary guest audience seated in her bedroom. "Ladies and gentlemen, please welcome the world renown Riz," she said loudly. "On today's show, Riz will discuss the latest fashions with the world's No. 1 supermodel, " she continued, giggling.

"You know," Deb said while in a yoga position near Riz, "you can't giggle like that if you want people to take you seriously."

"I know, but it's funny. One day my audience will be packed and then, who cares if I giggle as long as I look good." She giggled again.

"Riz, there's a lot more to know about the entertainment industry then just what looks good," Deb replied and stretched herself into the tree pose while closing her eyes.

Riz dismissed her with a ceremonial, "UMF!" and rolled her eyes. Further ignoring Deb, she went back to introducing herself into the mirror above the dresser.

As the dinosaurs grew bigger, Joan made all of their clothes by hand. Periodically, she'd measure each of them for new outfits. The boys were easy. So too was Deb for that matter. But, Riz was a different story.

Riz always asked her mother to purchase new fabrics for her when she went into town. Her preference was for fabrics with flowers on them. The problem was, Joan needed a lot of fabric to clothe a triceratops like Riz, and it was costly. Consequently, the arguments between Joan and Riz about clothing seemed never ending. Braun and Trex were easy because they wore jeans and shirts with jackets they altered to their individual liking. Deb always preferred her clothes more tailored to her body and comfortable.

Joan and Clem also made special shoes for the dinosaurs. The soles contained imprints of their initials so that they left tracks in the desert dirt wherever they went. That way, if they got lost, Joan and Clem could retrace their steps and find them.

Healthy food was always plentiful in the Stone household, lots of healthy food. Joan loved to cook and knew that eating healthy was necessary to protect her kids from getting sick, now or into their adult futures. She emphasized eating fruits, vegetables, whole grains, and protein and drinking lots of water while avoiding sugars, trans fats, white flour, soda, and junk food.

Deb was also adamant about eating right and often took over in Joan's absence to oversee what the others ate. Trex was on board because he knew that healthy eating helped maximize his performance while exercising.

Riz ate healthy too, but it didn't come as easy to her as it did to the others. She longed to visit one of the fast food restaurants advertised on television and to sink her big teeth into a fat, juicy hamburger with fries.

And, then there was Braun. Despite all of Joan's teachings regarding food, he seemed born with cravings for certain thing that humans can't eat. For example, Braun liked to munch on rocks, a habit of his that Joan, Clem, and the other three dinosaurs continuously tried to break.

Regardless of what the four dinosaurs ate, they ate lots of it. Carrying in the groceries was a real chore and all had to participate in order to get the job done. None seemed to mind because each was forever hungry. Joan and Clem had four more mouths to feed now, big mouths that never seemed satisfied.

When the four dinosaur kids were really young, it became apparent that they would grow bigger then average humans but remain smaller then their actual dinosaur ancestors. Clem

believed that this would occur because their eggs had mixed
with the earth's chemistry for millions and millions of years
and, consequently, their growth had been stunted. So, no,
they wouldn't grow to the actual size of their dinosaur ancestors. But, yes, they would be bigger than human beings. And,
it wasn't long before they stood taller and bigger than either
of their parents.

Because of their body frames and potential size, the
dinosaurs realized that they would never be able to do certain
things that other kids did. Although they didn't like to talk
about it, it made them sad. For example, they would never be
able to drive a car because their tails would get in the way.
They would never be able to ride on a roller coaster or an
airplane. They wouldn't be able to balance well on a regular
bicycle. The clothes they wore, although made for them
lovingly by Joan, were different than the clothes other kids
wore. They couldn't wear cool sneakers like other kids
because there wasn't a pair on the planet that would fit their
huge feet.

But, rather than look at life based on all that they couldn't
do, the dinosaurs decided to concentrate on what they could
do. With this outlook on life, they quickly realized they were
truly blessed in many, many ways. They celebrated their
uniqueness. They learned to do their best and forget the rest.

Gradually, their sadness over not being just like human kids went away.

Frequently, Joan and Clem took their children outside to teach them games that every kid in the United States plays. These delightful times were a lot of fun for the entire family.

One of their favorite games was baseball. The Stones divided into two teams, the boys against the girls. Trex, Braun, and Clem played against Joan, Riz, and Deb. So as not to suffer unnecessarily in the stifling daytime desert heat, they usually started their games around 5:00 p.m. when the sun was not so high in the sky. It was on one such hot, dry night of Stone baseball that Joan and Clem realized for the first time that each of their children possessed special super-powers.

"Okay, Trex, you're up," Clem said standing on second base, rocking back and forth, just waiting to run to third.

Trex walked up to home plate and stood poised like a statue. Lifting the bat, he stared fiercely into Joan's eyes as if this was the most important at bat in the final game of the World Series. Joan covered her face with her glove and turned to give Deb on first base and Riz in the shortstop position a look. Then she threw the ball toward home plate. Trex swung with all his might. He hit the ball poorly and it grounded slowly down the field between first and second base. Trex took off running to first while Deb scooted over to grab the moving ball. Just as she tried to pick it up, she kicked it by accident, sending it into the outfield. Trex kept running and almost collided with Deb. Except, when he got to where Deb was on the baseline, Trex jumped right over her. Clem had already started to run to third and as he passed Riz, he heard her scream.

"WHAT IS HE DOING?" Riz yelled. All she could see was Trex jumping higher and higher as he jumped onto second base and then to third, never taking any steps in between each base.

Deb finally grabbed the ball and ran with tremendous speed to catch up with her jumping brother. As she passed Joan on the pitcher's mound, Deb's speed was so intense, it blew Joan off her feet.

Riz was freaking out. All she could see was a cloud of smoke running at her and Trex jumping toward home plate. Joan was lying on the ground in complete shock.

"BONE-A-FIDE!" Braun yelled, indicating that he thought Trex and Deb's actions were really cool.

"STOP," Riz called out as a cloud of dust and a jumping Trex bounded toward her. All of a sudden, everything came to a complete stop. The dirt and dust settled.

"Deb, I couldn't even see you while you were running. It was like you were a bolt of lighting," yelled Riz.

"Both of you surprise me," exclaimed Joan. "Where did you get those jumping abilities, Trex?"

"I don't know. I didn't want to hit Deb and I wanted to get around all the bases as quickly as I could," Trex replied.

"Okay, Trex, let's see it again," Clem said.

Trex started running, threw his hands back, and jumped. He continued jumping upward until he was barely visible high in the sky. He looked like a spec of dust shooting upwards.

"Now that's what I call jumping," Braun exclaimed. "BONE-A-FIDE!"

Joan and Clem stared at each other in wide-eyed amazement.

"I bet I could catch up to him." Deb said as she took off running like the speed of light. Miraculously, in about two seconds, Trex and Deb were both standing back on the field with their family.

"Well, Trex, your jumping ability is amazing. Deb, your speed is unbelievable," Clem said.

"Oh yeah, Dad, you think my jumping is something? Watch this." Trex walked over to the side of the house and turned his entire body hard as a rock.

"What's happening to you?" questioned Riz.

"I've turned myself hard as a rock. Now, nothing can break through me," Trex yelled triumphantly. NOTHING."

"What?" asked Braun, staring in amazement at Trex. "Come on."

"Not only can I jump, but I can also turn hard as a rock and NOTHING can break through me," Trex explained again.

"Oh yeah, watch this," Riz huffed. All of a sudden, she charged at Trex. Just then, Trex moved out of the way and Riz charged right through the thick, heavy stucco wall of their house. Everyone looked at each other.

"I'm okay, I'm okay" Riz yelled from inside the settling dust engulfing the hole in the wall of the house.

"You may be OK, but what about our house," Joan screamed.

Turning, Joan and Clem looked over at their home that now had a huge hole in its side. Finally, Riz poked her big thorny head out through the hole and gave them all a thumb's up.

"That's one for the Riz, wouldn't you say?" she yelled while walking back to join the family.

"Do all of you have special powers we don't know about?" Clem asked surveying his four super-sized kids. Then, as if a cloud had been lifted, Trex, Deb, Riz, and Braun confessed how each one of them possessed special and unique powers. Before today, they'd been afraid to let their parents in on their little secret.

"Dad, you saw my powers today. I can jump really high and also turn hard as a rock. I can stop anything in my path," Trex volunteered excitedly.

"What can you do Braun?" Joan asked.

"That is, besides say BONE-A-FIDE!" piped in Deb sarcastically.

Very slowly and methodically Braun answered. "Well I am very, very strong and my brute strength is ... well, it's incredible. I've even lifted cars off the ground in your repair shop, Dad, when you weren't looking." Clem gasped.

"Yes, I've been there when he's done it. It's really cool," Deb said. "Dad, don't you remember the day you went into the shop and kept asking who'd been playing around with that blue '55 Chevy you'd been working on?"

"Yes."

"Well that was the day Braun lifted the Chevy over his head and all the stuff you were working on under the hood got a little out of place," Deb continued. "We all tried to help Braun put the stuff back where it belonged, but I know we missed a lot of things." Braun put his head down, so as to avoid his father's eyes.

"Well, what else can you four do? I think it's time you all confessed to your mother and me. Now, let's hear it," Clem asked calmly, not reprimanding Braun.

So, it was on a night of routine baseball that the Stones first learned the details of their children's unique qualities and superpowers.

Riz explained that she can inhale large amounts of water, even an entire lake, and exhale it to help put out fires. She can also charge and break through anything.

"We all believe you, Riz. Look what you just did to our house," Joan said, somewhat frustrated.

Deb explained that she can run faster then anyone and outrun any moving object on earth, even a high-speed train. And, while she's at it, she can run on any surface, even vertical structures like the sides of a building. She can also break glass by screeching. When she tilts the bone on the back of her head as far back as possible, she makes a high-pitched noise that will shatter glass.

Trex can jump unbelievably high and he can turn hard as a rock. Braun can catapult things with his huge tail and his brute strength is remarkable.

To illustrate his ability to catapult, Braun suddenly put his tail down around Deb, scooped her up into it, and tossed her more than three hundred yards onto the roof of their home, loudly yelling "BONE-A-FIDE" as Deb soared through the air.

Jostled, Deb finally got her footing on the rooftop and screamed angrily, "That's enough, Braun. We all believed you when you told us you could catapult things with your tail. Don't ever do that to me again or I'll screech in your big ears and shatter your. ..."

"Enough, enough," yelled Clem. None of you will ever use your superpowers to hurt each other. Do you hear me?"

"Yes, we hear you, Dad," they all responded, almost in perfect unison.

Joan and Clem looked at each other in amazement. Their four kids were indeed different. Each had special and unique powers. No two were the same. It seemed that, beyond baseball, they were a great team that could help each other out in a pinch. What had started out as just another game of baseball had turned into one very informative, magical evening.

Finally, Clem turned to the group and said, "OK, so now we know things about each of you that we never knew before. But, I know one other thing too. We all must help cover that hole in the wall that Riz just created. Let's get moving. It's already pretty dark out here. We don't want any little desert animals crawling through that hole in the wall tonight, now do we?"

And so, in the blink of an eye, the four dinosaurs who wanted nothing more than to be like human kids, let it be known that they possessed superpowers that other kids didn't have. But, in many ways, they were just like all the other kids in the world. Although super-sized, their daily life involved schoolwork, playtime, meals, sports, TV, the Internet, and all the other things most kids do.

There was one other thing, though, that further set these dinosaurs apart from other kids. They were terribly afraid of ice. Yes, ice. Just plain ice that you find in your freezer or that you skate on in the winter when the pond freezes over or that sometimes covers the surface of the road, especially at night. Regardless of where ice was located, these dinosaurs wanted no part of it. Can you imagine that?

Why did they fear ice? Because they believed that it was the ice age that took the lives of their biological parents and other dinosaur ancestors. So, ice was their enemy and they avoided it in all situations. They wouldn't have ice cubes in their drinks. They would not go near a freezer. They never ice skated or watched hockey games on television.

Worst of all, they wouldn't eat ice cream. No chocolate, vanilla, or strawberry. They never tasted ice cream with birthday cake. Imagine never watching ice cream melt down around a slice of birthday cake on your plate? Imagine never tasting the sweetness of the sugar from the frosting as it blends in with the sweetness of the ice cream and explodes in your mouth? It tastes soooooooooo good! But, these dinosaurs didn't know that. Nor did they care. Simply put, they wanted nothing to do with ice, regardless of whether or not it was their birthday.

CHAPTER 8

A Very Special Birthday Present

As their tenth birthday approached, all four dinosaurs got really excited in anticipation of the presents they'd get from their parents. After all, a tenth birthday is a very special event. Forget about the cake. They wanted presents.

"I can't wait until next week, Deb, can you?" asked Riz as all four dinosaurs gathered in Clem's workshop late one afternoon when their parents were off grocery shopping.

"No, I can't. What do you think Mom and Dad are going to give us?" responded Trex.

"I don't know. All I hope is that it's something with flowers on it."

Braun looked up from underneath the hood of a car he was working on. He gave Riz a cold stare and said, "Flowers on it? What are you talking about, Riz? Do you think that just because you like flowers, we all do? I for one don't want anything with flowers on it. Not for my birthday. Not ever."

"Good for you, Braun. Who said anything about all of us getting the same gift? I'm only talking about what I want," Riz shot back.

"What's new? That's pretty much all you ever talk about anyway," Deb said.

Just then, they heard the sound of their parents' truck approaching. "Looks like it's time to end this conversation right now, what d'ya say?" Trex asked.

"I agree. Let's give it a rest," Braun replied.

Clem and Joan yelled out to the dinosaurs to come help carry in the groceries. All four of them bolted outside. The bed of the truck was packed with grocery bags and cases of bottled water and Dino-Ade. It took an awful lot of drinks to quench their mighty thirsts in the desert heat.

Quickly, with all of them helping, the task was complete. The groceries were safely inside. Trex and Deb stayed in the kitchen and helped Joan put everything away. Braun carried the duplicate items into the garage and stored them in the family's second refrigerator that stood against the back wall. Riz was already breaking open a bag of trail mix and popping a can of Dino-Ade.

That night, after eating dinner and watching TV, Trex and Braun went to their bedroom, a room that was getting pretty crowded as the two of them grew. After the lights were out,

Braun spoke. "By this same time next week, we'll know what our birthday gifts are. Not too much longer."

And so, on the following Tuesday, after they had all eaten an early morning breakfast of fresh fruit and bran cereal, Joan and Clem gathered the four bulky dinosaurs in the living room. Three of them squeezed onto the large sectional couch. Trex lay on the floor.

"As you know, today's a very special day. It's your tenth birthday!"

Each of the dinosaurs' eyes lit up with excitement as Clem spoke. They nodded agreement with his statement, eagerly anticipating their gifts.

"Your mother and I have something very special planned for you today," Clem continued. "We've been planning this surprise for some time now."

Joan continued where Clem left off. "We've never taken you back to the place where we found your eggs. We thought that we'd do that today."

Riz, Trex, Deb, and Braun looked at each other. Something was going on. None of them could see any brightly wrapped gifts nearby. Maybe there were none. They wanted real gifts, not a trip in the desert.

"So, let's get going. You can all squeeze into the truck bed. I've packed a picnic lunch. Let's all go explore the cave where Dad and I found your eggs."

The dinosaurs' looks of disappointment and lack of enthusiasm for Joan's suggestion were obvious to their parents. Finally, Clem spoke. "Wait. Before we go, I've got something for each of you."

He went into the hall closet and brought out four identically wrapped presents, each the same size, just a little bigger than a shoebox. "Here, before we go, open these." Since none of the packages had nametags on them, it didn't matter which dinosaur got which box.

Braun was the first to get into his box and he lifted out a pair of goggles. He held them up and twirled them around by the head strap as his sisters and brother extracted identical goggles from their boxes.

"Goggles? What are these? They can't be for swimming. Not much of that going on out here in the desert," Braun said, trying not to sound too disappointed.

"Son, these aren't just ordinary goggles. I've spent many hours inventing them for all of you. Put them on and see what you see."

All did as Clem said. Trex walked to the living room window and looked out.

"I can't believe it! I can't believe it!" he shouted.

"What can't you believe, Trex?" asked Braun, ambling over toward the big window himself.

By the time Braun got there, Deb and Riz were already looking out. Each yelled at the top of their lungs.

"Is this cool or what?" shouted Riz.

"How'd you do this, Dad? Is this a trick or something?" asked Deb.

When Braun finally looked through his goggles at the outside landscape, his knees buckled and he almost fell to the ground. "Dad, I see dinosaurs out there. Real, live dinosaurs, lots of them."

"That's right, Braun. That's exactly what I'd hope you'd see."

"But, how'd you do this, Dad? How the heck did you make these goggles? Where are these dinosaurs I'm seeing? Are they real or is it a movie playing inside the goggles?"

"No, the dinosaurs you're seeing are real dinosaurs from the past. These goggles let you look back into the past and see the landscape exactly as it was in prehistoric times when dinosaurs actually roamed the earth. In fact, you're probably looking at some of your very own ancestors right now."

"BONE-A-FIDE!" screamed Braun, "BONE-A-FIDE!"

"That's amazing, Dad. Amazing. You're so smart," Riz said.

"I'm just glad the goggles work for you. Now, we all have a very important mission to go on today. We're going back to the cave where we found you and see what else may be inside that cave. With the help of your new goggles, you should see a lot more than your mother or I can."

"Dad, what are these goggles called?" asked Deb.

"GEOGOGS," Clem replied.

"Does anyone else have a pair of GEOGOGS?" Riz asked.

"No, they don't, Riz. No one else in the world has GEO-GOGS. Let's just keep it a secret among ourselves, OK?" Clem said.

"It's OK by me," Riz continued. "These are so cool. I can't wait to see what we find in the cave."

So, off the family went to find the cave of the dinosaurs' origin. Now, all four of the dinosaurs were much more excited about the trip because they were each equipped with a pair of new GEOGOGS.

After parking the truck at the base of the mountain, the family started the steep trek up to the cave entrance. It was a slow, tiring trip. When they were about a hundred yards from the entrance, Braun put on his GEOGOGS. Suddenly, he froze in his tracks.

Before him was a huge dinosaur with a massive purple shawl tied around its neck exiting the cave. For a moment, the dinosaur stopped in its tracks and looked back into the cave. When he turned forward again, Braun saw big tears glistening in his eyes. Suddenly, he came out of the cave and started running down the mountain on the same path that Braun and his family were on right now. Huge boulders flew off the footpath on which he ran. Quickly, Braun removed his GEOGOGS.

"Dad, Dad. I see a humongous dinosaur headed right for us on this path."

"Don't worry, Braun. He's not really here now. You're seeing something that occurred many millions of years ago. That's the special power of the GEOGOGS. They take you back in time."

"Thank goodness, Dad. That's one big fellow. He scares the pants off me," responded Braun as Trex, Riz, and Deb put their goggles on to see what all the excitement was about.

"Yikes! You're right. He's coming right at us!" shrieked Deb. "Let's get out of here mucho pronto."

"Calm down. Calm down. Remember, he's not really here right now," Clem said again.

Finally, the family arrived at the cave entrance and walked inside. After just seeing the big guy from the past on the footpath with their GEOGOGS, the dinosaurs weren't at all sure that this was something they really wanted to do.

When prodded to do so by their parents, all four entered the cave. Riz and Deb held hands. Braun hung back using the excuse that his enormous size might get in the way of the others as they tried to move into the cave. Trex put his arm around his mother and steered her inside. Clem led the way, lantern in hand.

Soon, they arrived in the area of the cave where Joan and Clem had found their eggs ten years ago.

"Here we are. Put on your GEOGOGS and let us know what you see," Clem said.

"What about you, Dad? Don't you and Mom have a pair of GEOGOGS too?" Trex asked.

"No, we don't, Trex. And, even if we did, I'm not sure we'd see what you are able to see."

The dinosaurs cautiously put on their GEOGOGS and carefully surveyed the portion of the cave where they were standing. Deb was the first to speak.

"I see something coming up out of the floor over there. It looks like it could be a very big egg," she said.

"Where?" asked Clem.

"Over there, Dad, near that odd rock formation in the corner."

Clem looked in the direction Deb pointed but couldn't see anything. "I don't see a thing, Deb."

"Then, the GEOGOGS are really working, Dad," chimed in Trex. "I see it too."

All of the dinosaurs moved to the spot on the cave floor where they could see the big egg through their GEOGOGS. When they took off the GEOGOGS, they saw nothing there either.

"I think we have to dig a little," Braun said. "It seems like the egg is actually a few feet down under the dirt. That's what we're seeing through our goggles."

"Well, let's get going, then," Riz ordered. "Let's get going pretty quick. This place is starting to freak me out."

Clem came over to the spot where they all stood and helped dig in the dirt. It wasn't long before they reached a smooth, curved surface at the bottom of the hole they made.

"Stop digging and go slowly," cautioned Joan. "If it's another egg, don't break it."

They obeyed Joan. Working slowly and with great care, eventually they extracted a huge egg from the dirt.

"Another egg," exclaimed Joan. "Let's take it home with us. Maybe it's another dinosaur."

"You may be right, Joan. What do you all think? Should we bring it home and see if this egg turns into a new little brother or sister for the four of you?" Clem asked.

"I'm game," responded Riz excitedly.

"Me too. I'll even help change its diapers," Deb said.

"OK, OK. We just can't leave it here, now can we?" asked Trex.

"I say we take it home. End of discussion. Let's get moving," barked big brother Braun. "What are you all waiting for?"

"Wait, I see something else down in the hole," Trex said while looking through his GEOGOGS.

"What is it?" Braun asked.

"It looks like some type of an odd shaped stick. Wait, it's got something bright red on one end of it. Let me get it."

Trex reached into the hole and pulled out the stick. He examined it carefully as his parents and siblings looked over his shoulders.

"I don't know what this is, but I'm going to keep it. Check out this red crystal on the end of it. One thing's for sure, it has some connection to the dinosaurs of the past. And, most likely, since our eggs were found in this same cave, it has some direct connection to each of us too. From now on, it'll be my magic stick," Trex said proudly.

"Whatever! Looks like nothing more than a bent stick to me," Riz muttered.

"I'd say that your magic stick, the egg, and this whole cave are BONE-A-FIDE! What do you think Deb?" Braun asked.

"I think that this is a very special place but I'm sick of hearing you say BON..." Deb started to say.

"No more of that, you two. We've got work to do in order to get this egg home without breaking it. Please, Deb. Please don't make that high-pitched shrieking noise of yours. That alone could break the egg," Joan said.

So the Stone family gathered up the stuff they found in the cave and headed home. The four dinosaurs were tired after a very long day. But, it had been a very special birthday for them. Not only did they each get a pair of magical GEO-GOGS, they may also have found a new brother or sister.

Joan did the exact same thing with the new egg that she'd done with the original four.

She placed it in a padded bowl under a plant lamp on the shelf in her kitchen. And, just as had happened before, in a couple of weeks, the egg cracked open. This time, it happened while the entire family was gathered at their evening meal. When they heard the cracking noise, all jumped up from the table and ran to the plant shelf.

There, peeking out of the broken eggshell was another tiny dinosaur.

"I think it's just like me, Dad. It's a tyrannosaur. Don't you think so?" Trex asked excitedly.

Clem delicately picked the baby dinosaur up and examined it. "Yes, it is, Trex. And, it's a boy. You all have a new little brother," Clem proclaimed while looking at Joan.

"A boy! That's wonderful," Joan exclaimed, clasping her hands together in front of her.

"What shall we name him?" Clem asked.

"If you don't mind, I'd like to name him," Trex said. "After all, he and I are the same species. Actually, maybe we're even related in some way."

"It's OK with me," Braun said quickly.

"Me too," offered Deb.

"Go for it," Riz cheered.

"Your father and I agree, Trex. You should name him," Joan said.

"Then, it's all set. I want to call him Little T. How's that sound?" Trex asked, waving his magic stick over the new baby.

"That's fine, Trex. That's fine. Little T it is," Clem said.

At the exact same time Little T was born, Dr. Dimitri Roy, at home in Chicago between dinosaur digs, was grocery shopping for himself and his bird. Suddenly, while in the dairy aisle, he began to experience the same type of seizure he'd experienced ten years earlier while on the fruitless dig in Montana. Uncontrollable flapping of his arms, legs, and head drew many people to him, all offering assistance. Then, he let out a huge roar that seemed too loud to come from his body. Many in the crowd that had gathered around him were frightened and began to move away.

"Call 911," shouted a brave soul in the crowd.

"No, don't call anyone. I know what this is," Dr. Roy lied. "I'm OK. I just need to take my medicine."

Quickly, he ran out of the store leaving all of his groceries in the cart in the diary aisle. He ran toward his bright mustard yellow tank-link SUV, easily recognizable in the

huge parking lot jammed with cars. As he approached, he
saw his bird snoozing with his head pressed against the front
passenger side window. When Dr. Roy flung open the driver
side front door, the bird was startled, flapped his wings, and
let out a loud shriek.

"Be quiet," snapped Dr. Roy. "Something is happening
that hasn't happened in ten years. I don't know what it is.
Let's hurry and get home as soon as we can." And, with that,
Dr. Roy and his bird sped off towards their Chicago home.

Back in Arizona, there were now five dinosaurs in the
Stone household. The birthday gift of the GEOGOGS had led
to the discovery of Little T's egg. But, it had also led to a
new pastime for the dinosaurs. They liked to look through
their GEOGOGS and see things humans could not see.
Because their goggles were so special and had taken so long
to make using secrets only Clem understood, he sternly
instructed his children not to lose their GEOGOGS.

To help the dinosaurs protect their goggles, Joan sewed
a secret compartment into all of their clothes to keep the
GEOGOGS safe when they weren't wearing them. The special compartments were in different places in each piece of
clothing they wore. Each dinosaur knew where the hiding
places were in their own clothing. Quickly, all of them
decided to call these secret hiding places, Gog Pockets. They
liked the fact that they had a special pocket in their clothing,

something other kids didn't have. They knew that they possessed something really, really special. They wondered what other kids would think if they knew about the existence of the GEOGOGS.

But, most of all, they wondered what other kids would think if they knew about their existence here on earth. What would other kids think if they knew that, yes, dinosaurs were really living among them.

In Chicago, Dr. Dimitri Roy wondered too. He wondered what in the world was going on with him. The roar he made during a seizure frightened even him. Where was it coming from? What caused it to happen? Would there be another episode? If so, when?

CHAPTER 9

Home Sweet Home

Once Little T arrived, the whole dynamic in the Stone household changed. As Trex, Braun, Deb, and Riz grew bigger and bigger, the Stones knew they had a problem on their hands. Trex, Braun, and Little T now crowded into the bedroom that had originally been Clem's TV room. Deb and Riz occupied and overwhelmed Joan's sewing room.

Plain and simple, the Stones' home was just not big enough for their growing, super-sized family. Clem and Joan had to figure out a solution to the space problem, and they needed to figure it out quickly and cost effectively.

"Couldn't we just add on to the back of the house near the family room, Clem?" Joan asked hopefully.

"No, we can't just add on. At this point, we don't even know for sure how big they'll all get," Clem said scratching his head. "Imagine if they grow into full-sized dinosaurs? If we think we've got problems now, look out!" Clem exclaimed as he continued to ponder how he could get more living space for the dinosaurs. He knew he needed to quickly take some action.

From the beginning, the entire family enjoyed having Little T around, especially Deb and Riz. They wrapped him with the towels Joan used as diapers. They brought him everywhere they went. Many times, Joan had to hunt him down to feed him.

"Riz, where is Little T?" Joan asked as she looked around the back yard after noticing Riz standing alone next to one of the big trash cans on the side of the hill.

"He's going for a ride right now. Why? Do you need him?" Riz yelled back.

"A ride?" Joan asked. "What kind of a ride?" And, just then she realized what was going on.

"Riz, is Little T inside that TRASH CAN?" Joan screamed.

Riz jumped when Joan yelled. She dropped the cover onto the trash can and lost her balance, hitting the side of the can ever so slightly as she fell. The impact of her body weight was just enough to tip the garbage can over. Instantly, it started to roll down the hill.

"GET HIM," yelled Joan, as she ran after the rolling can. "GET HIM."

Riz jumped up and started to run down the hill after the can, but she couldn't catch it. Trex heard all the yelling and ran outside just in time to see his mother chasing after the rolling trash can. He realized that she was trying to stop it, so he ran to the bottom of the hill. He let the can hit him and it stopped abruptly. Trex lifted his magic stick up over his head to signify his success in stopping the can.

Joan arrived where Trex was standing at just about the same time he stopped the can. She hurriedly opened the lid and saw Little T inside looking up with those big eyes of his and smiling. Quickly, she scooped him up into her arms and, patting his head, asked, "Are you OK, little guy? Are you OK?" She shot an angry look at Riz while comforting Little T.

"Don't ever do that again, Riz! Do you understand me? He's your brother. He's not a toy? He could have gotten hurt," Joan said firmly.

Riz nodded agreement and then looked at Little T. He smiled back at her. If Riz hadn't known better, she'd have sworn he was saying with his eyes, "That was a lot of fun, Sis. Let's do it again."

Little T grew fast and he, more than all the others, enjoyed being a daredevil. In fact, nothing scared him. He would try anything. Being the youngest, he always found things to occupy his time. He liked to play outside. He invented his own sports games and became a very good skateboarder. He never sat still for long. Schoolwork bored him. When he wasn't playing sports himself, he was getting the stats on his favorite teams and players off the Internet.

"Do you know who holds the record for the most consecutive games with a hit?" Little T asked everyone at the dinner table one night.

"Who cares?" said Riz, as she kept eating.

Trex looked up. "Who? Are you going to give us any clues? What team did he play for?".

"No, try and guess," responded Little T, looking at Clem for a sign of approval. Clem smiled and nodded at him. All of the dinosaurs remained silent.

"Well, guess it'll be my secret then," Little T said, a bit disappointed.

"OK. I've got one for you then," said Clem, "Do you know who says,

"I've seen better cuts in a meat market."

"C. Everett Stone," Braun replied slowly. Everyone looked up and started laughing. "We know that's one of your favorite expressions, Dad."

"Good job, Braun," Clem said. "Glad to see you're paying attention to me."

"Do you know what language Dad says it in?" Deb chimed in. Everyone looked at each other.

"ENGLISHHHHHHH," Little T yelled and everyone laughed even more.

From the beginning, Little T's superpowers were evident. Joan first noticed one of his powers when she wrapped him in his baby blanket. As she did so, he turned the exact color of the blanket. Little T was able to camouflage himself by turning his body into the color of his immediate surroundings, no matter what color (or colors) they were. As he aged, he also took on more and more of Trex's special powers. That made sense to Joan and Clem because both Trex and Little T were the same type of dinosaur, a tyrannosaur.

The five dinosaurs continued to enjoy life with their parents. Time seemed to fly by. Each day, Little T grew bigger and bigger until the house was definitely too small for the family to live in comfortably. It was obvious they had to do something and do it immediately.

Clem had been trying to find a solution for a couple of years now. Suddenly, one day, it came to him. He would build them their own house out behind the main house. Everything in it would be designed to accommodate their super sizes while still leaving room for them to grow.

So, for the next couple of months, Clem worked on constructing a house for the dinosaurs. He used heavy metal sheets and built a structure that resembled an airplane hanger. It was huge, with four sides and an arched top. The front looked like the front of the town garage. It had a big door that was tall enough and wide enough for the super-sized dinosaurs to get in and out of easily. On the back wall, about three quarters of the way up, there were several windows.

The construction work was hard and all of the Stones helped out. Some things were made easier because of the dinosaurs' special powers. For example, it was easy for Braun to lift the heavy pieces of metal into place. When his Dad was up on the scaffolding, he could catapult whatever tool he needed right to him. Trex could easily jump onto the roof and hammer nails with his big feet.

Day and night, work continued on their new building despite the extreme Arizona heat. When they got overheated, Riz inhaled gallons of water from the garden hose and sprayed all of them to cool them off. When they were hungry, Deb shot to their parents' house with the speed of a bullet and brought back lots of healthy food for them.

Once the outside of the building was complete, it was time to furnish the inside. Everyone had their own ideas of how the inside should look. Clem and Joan became skillful at finding everyday items and adapting them for the dinosaurs.

Clem salvaged five old trampolines from local schools and used them for the dinosaurs' beds. They easily accommodated the dinosaurs' sizes and were comfortable too. Joan covered them with blue crash mats so they weren't too bouncy.

In the bathroom, the dinosaurs used ice scrapers for tooth-brushes and each one used a full tube of toothpaste each and every day. For dental floss, they used thin nylon line, rolled and hung on the wall over the bathroom sink. For a toilet, Clem rigged an old claw-foot bathtub for the dinosaurs. He cut out a large piece of plywood in the shape of the top of the bathtub as a toilet seat and plumbed the whole contraption so it would flush like a regular toilet. For their shower, Clem hooked up an old car wash system on the outside of the building. Each day, they took turns walking through each of the stations in the carwash, including the big, rough, yellow brushes that surrounded them on both sides and scrubbed their scaly skin clean.

The kitchen table was an old cable spool covered with padding with smaller cable spools as chairs. A portion of the inside space was set aside for exercising. In fact, Clem found an old motorized airport walkway for sale online. He bought it right away and installed it as their treadmill.

Clem knew that Braun loved music and dancing. Deb and Riz did too. So, he installed one of those sparkling dance hall balls on the ceiling near the CD player. Clem found it on the Internet too.

A huge slide connected the second-floor loft to the living room. The dinosaurs loved to slide down it. Joan also designed computer workstations near the classroom area.

Little T, the dare devil, was adamant about building a ramp out in back so he could ride his skateboard. Finally, one day, Clem caved in to his demands. Trex, Braun, and Little T helped their father build him a half pipe. Once it was completed, Little T rode his board up and down and attempted extreme tricks every day of the week.

One day, Little T decided that it would be fun to have Braun stand about three hundred yards away and catapult him onto his skate-board perched on top of his half pipe. Then, he'd skate down the ramp. So, he begged and begged Braun until he agreed.

"OK, Little T, just sit down on my tail and wrap your arms around the end," Braun said with some hesitation. He was scared that if this did not work, they would both be grounded for a long time, maybe a couple of years. He knew that, regardless, he'd get the worst of it because he was older and should have known better.

"Braun, flip me as high as you can. Do it with all your might. Just aim at my skateboard," persisted Little T.

Braun sighed. Trex, standing nearby, shook his head signifying that this was not a good idea and simultaneously pounded his magic stick into the ground for extra emphasis.

Finally, Braun took a deep breath, so deep the nearby cactus moved when he exhaled. Using all of his strength, he flipped Little T into the air.

Little T started to fly through the air. It didn't take long for both Braun and Trex to realize that this definitely wasn't a good idea. But by that time, it was too late. Little T was flying away from them. And, he was flying fast. Up, up and away!

Trex screamed, "You threw him too hard. He's going to end up in California."

As Braun and Trex looked up, Little T flew right up and over the half pipe. Immediately, he was really far away and flying with great speed.

"Come on, Trex, we've got to do something, and do it now," Braun ordered as he started to run in the direction Little T was flying.

Trex jumped high in the sky right toward the diminishing object that was his little brother. As he rose up in the sky, he held his magic stick tightly in his right hand.

Riz and Deb heard all the commotion and ran outside to see what was going on.

"Why are you guys yelling?" asked Deb. But it was too late. Braun was barely visible in the distance, running toward the mountains to the west. Trex continued to bounce higher and higher into the sky, turning and flapping his magic stick as he jumped.

"Wait up, guys. What happened?" the girls yelled simultaneously.

When no one answered, Deb and Riz looked at each other and, in the blink of an eye, took off running after their brothers.

"Deb, I can't run that fast," exclaimed Riz, breathing heavily as she stomped alongside Deb. "Just go ahead. I'll catch up."

With that, Deb took off running with the speed of a jet-propelled rocket. Within nanoseconds, Riz could no longer see her. So, Riz took it upon herself to stop running and rest for a while. Finally, she took off again and ultimately caught up with Trex, Braun, and Deb, all of whom had by then successfully retrieved Little T from his flight in the sky.

"What happened?" Riz asked.

"Well, Braun catapulted me up in the air using his tail and I flew off just like a jet plane. It was so cool. I was flying so high. I think I was on my way to California. That is until Trex jumped up and grabbed me and brought me back down to earth," Little T answered excitedly.

"WHAT!" Riz yelled.

"I tried to flip him up onto the half pipe, but my tail got a little carried away," Braun said apologetically.

"Come on, Braun. You know better than that. Dad's going to be very angry," Riz yelled.

"I know. I know. But, just think. For a minute we almost had our own airline," Little T joked.

"No more. It's nothing to laugh about. You take too many risks," Trex said, pointing at Little T with his magic stick. With that, the entire group headed for home as Riz once again huffed and puffed.

"Let's not tell Mom and Dad, OK?" asked Little T. "Let's not upset them."

"OK, it's our secret, all of ours," responded Braun as he looked around to all of his brothers and sisters each of whom silently nodded agreement.

Joan and Clem had a big surprise waiting for the dinosaurs when they got home. They met up with them at the entrance to the dinosaurs' home.

"Well, it's taken us a long time. But, together, we've turned this place into a pretty nice home for you guys. Don't you agree?" Clem asked.

"Of course, Dad. It's the best," Riz said.

"Then, we've got a special surprise for all of you. Your mother and I decided that this place needed a name, not just the "back house" as we've been calling it. So, from now on, it will be known as the Bone Zone. What do you think of that?"

"That's great. I like it," Little T volunteered.

"Come inside, there's more," Joan said as she slowly pushed the big, heavy doors open so all could enter.

The dinosaurs all saw the sign at the same time. It hung on the back wall and was made up of long bones spelling the words, "Bone Zone." Clem's old friend, an iron-worker, had helped him design and build the sign thinking it was for a chic new restaurant in Scottsdale.

"I love it. We live in the Bone Zone! The Bone Zone!" chanted Deb.

"How cool is that?" asked Trex.

"I'd say it's really cool, Trex. In fact, I'd say it's BONE-A-FIDE!" said Braun emphatically.

"Glad you all like it. Now let's all clean up for dinner," Clem said. "We'll meet you back here in about ten minutes. Mom has cooked a great meal to celebrate the Bone Zone."

When dinner was done and the dinosaurs had all cleaned up, they headed for their beds in the Bone Zone. Trex and Little T had a bedroom on the left side of the Bone Zone. Directly across on the opposite side of the building, Riz and Deb slept in their room. Braun's room was right next to Riz and Deb. He needed more room than the others because of his big tail. Like most brothers and sisters, they argued about whose "stuff" was where. If they found someone else's "stuff" in their space, they'd yell, "Get it off my side."

Riz's bedding was decorated with flowers. A mirror with the same print as the bedding hung next to her bed. Deb's bed had a more classic line to it. Her bedding was a muted orange color. Two posters, one of yoga positions and one of karate moves, hung next to her bed. Little T's area was decorated in camouflage. His skateboard, stale food, and dirty clothes were usually strewn all over. Trex's side of the room was far neater and his bed was covered with a blue and white checkered bedspread. He had a special place in the corner where he leaned his magic stick when he slept. Braun's bedroom had a baseball theme. Over his bed, a big "B" made of baseball bats hung in honor of the Boston Red Sox. And, because he absolutely loved island music, he had a plastic, blow-up palm tree with tiny white lights on it nestled in the corner of his room.

Trex found little humor in having Little T's stuff overflow onto his side of the room.

"Little T, I'm not kidding. Get your smelly socks off my bed," Trex yelled, prodding at the socks with his magic stick.

"They're not just my socks. They're a science experiment. I'm trying to see if they can actually get so dirty that they'll walk away all by themselves. Mom told me that would happen if I didn't pick them up and put them in the laundry," Little T explained.

"Oh, you think they'll actually walk away all by themselves? Well, while you're running your little experiment, why don't you take it OUTSIDE and sleep with it out there. While you're at it, watch out for coyotes," joked Trex.

Riz laughed but she stopped laughing when Little T suddenly grabbed his smelly socks, shot across the Bone Zone, and threw them onto her bed.

"Ewwwww! Get them off my bed," Riz shrieked.

Riz grabbed the filthy socks with only two fingers so as to barely touch them and flung them onto Deb's bed. Trex, Little T, and Riz all started laughing as they stared at the socks. Just then, Deb walked in from outside and saw the socks lying on her bed. Her facial expression quickly turned from one of curiosity to one of anger.

"Who put those gross socks on my bed?" Deb yelled, sniffing the foul odor that now filled her bedroom.

"Little T did," Riz exploded laughing. Little T, sensing that he was about to get into trouble, quickly grabbed his skate-board. As he tried to skate past her toward the kitchen, Deb grabbed his arm and flung him back onto her bed.

"Aren't you forgetting something, my little friend?" Deb asked pointing to his gross, smelly socks lying on her bed. Little T grabbed his socks and threw them over the wall into Braun's room. Although they all knew that Braun was in his room, he didn't say anything as the smelly socks tumbled in.

Trex, Riz, Deb, and Little T waited expecting to hear something from Braun. Two minutes went by and still he said nothing. Trex tiptoed toward Braun's room and peeked around the wall.

As he turned his head back toward his baby brother and sisters, he whispered, "Shhhh, he's sleeping. They landed right in the middle of his stomach, but he's still sleeping. Sooner or later he'll smell them. That'll wake him up for sure."

Everyone laughed. Then, one by one, they each tiptoed off in a different direction toward their own comfy bed in the Bone Zone. Each expected to hear rumblings from Braun sometime during the night, especially Little T, who was determined to become the world's first "sock scientist!"

www.thefossibles.com

CHAPTER 10

Are There Cars in Their Stars?

As the dinosaurs got older, it was more and more difficult to obey their parents' rule of not letting human beings see them or learn of their existence. All of them longed to enjoy the things human teenagers did, especially to drive a car. Joan and Clem sensed their growing frustration and knew that they must do something soon or the dinosaurs might disobey them.

"Joan, don't you think the kids are getting impatient now that they're getting older?" Clem asked and, without waiting for Joan's response, continued. "I get a strong feeling that the outside world is calling to them. They've seen so much on TV and the Internet. Seems to me, they're chomping at the bit to get a taste of what real life is like out there," he said pointing in the direction of the bright lights of downtown Phoenix nestled in the Valley of the Sun.

"I know, Clem. Braun is especially worrisome to me. You know how much he loves cars. Well, yesterday he asked me if I thought there was a car that he could fit into. He's so anxious to drive."

"What'd you tell him?"

"I tried to go easy on him because I know he's very self-conscious about his big tail. But, honestly, Clem, you know he can't fit into any car or truck they make today. I told him so as delicately as I could. But I also said that maybe there was something else he could drive, something that he'd be comfortable riding in."

"What might that be? If Braun can't fit into any car or truck they make today, what CAN he drive?"

"Well, that's where you come in. Why can't he drive a motorcycle, a motorcycle you build just for him?"

"What? Do you have any idea how big that motorcycle would have to be, Joan?"

"Yes, I think I do. But, why not give it a try? You've built some pretty outrageous bikes for your customers. Why not build one for your own son?"

"But that huge tail, what would I have to build to take care of that tail?"

"I'm sure you will think of something, Clem. You're good at things like that.

Anyway, from where I'm standing, if it's a choice between building him a motorcycle or risking him walking out into the real world and getting captured, I vote for the motorcycle."

"Come on. You know that I don't want him to get captured any more than you do." Clem hesitated for only a few seconds and then continued, "OK. I'll make a rough sketch of a bike for him and see what you think of it."

"While you're at it, there's one more thing," Joan said.

"What's that?"

"We can't just build a motorcycle for Braun. They all want to drive. Even Little T."

"You mean you want me to build each of them a motorcycle," Clem exclaimed.

"Yes, that's exactly what I mean."

"Well, if that's the path we're going down, I'll need some help. Actually, they all might enjoy participating in building their own bike. Do you think we should ask them before we get started?"

"Yes. Yes. That's a great idea."

"Then, let's go over to the Bone Zone right now and have a little discussion with them. I bet they'll all be very excited," Clem said.

And so, on the night Clem and Joan first told the dinosaurs about the motorcycles, if you were in outer space, miles and miles up in the sky over the Arizona desert, you would have heard their screams of joy. For miles around, small desert animals ran for shelter as the loud noises the dinosaurs made ricocheted off the stark boulders. A seismograph at the weather station in downtown Phoenix registered a 5.0 on the Richter scale. Scientists swarmed around the device and determined upon further inspection that it must have been a simple malfunction. After all, they detected no shifts in the earth's surface in and around Phoenix.

"Shh, shh," Joan cautioned, as the dinosaurs yelled and heavily pounded their big feet on the ground. "Be quiet. Someone will hear you and they may come to investigate."

"Bring it on!" Braun said, pumping up his chest, full of uncharacteristic bluster now that he was going to get his own motorcycle. "That's what I say. Bring it on!"

"Stop, Braun. That's exactly what we don't want. We're building these bikes to keep you safe, not to yell to the world that you exist and live out here in the desert."

"OK. OK, Mom," Braun responded. "I understand."

Nonetheless, the five dinosaurs were ecstatic. Each of them was getting their own motorcycle. What more could they ask? They had the best parents in the whole wide world.

Clem spent a couple of days sketching possible bike designs and then he met again with all of the dinosaurs.

"Look, I was thinking about your bikes. It seems to me that we ought to build them so they're really unique. After all, you ARE dinosaurs! So, I thought it would be really cool to use old bones we scavenge in the desert for handlebars and things. What do you think of that?"

"I like that idea, Dad," piped in Trex.

"Me too, Dad. That sounds cool," Little T replied.

"Yeah, but are the bones going to be all yucky?" Riz asked. "I don't want to have handlebars with goobers all over them."

"No, Riz. They'll be all cleaned off and smoothed over. Here's what they'll look like," Clem said. He pulled a big white bone from a burlap bag beside him on the floor and held it up. "See. They look just like the bones in the Bone Zone sign."

"Oh, that's OK, Dad. That's OK as long as my bike can have flowers on it somewhere," Riz said.

"Your bike can have whatever design you want on it, Riz. Now, if you are all in agreement, I'll use bones for some of the structural components. OK?" Clem asked one more time.

"I think it's OK with all of us, Dad," Deb said. "Trex, do you agree? You're the only one who hasn't said anything yet."

"Yeah, I agree. As long as my bike has a place to carry my magic stick, it's OK with me," Trex replied.

"OK. Then we need to get busy and start building. Oh, one more thing, I'm going to deck the bikes out with all the latest in electronics, some I've made especially for you.

Right now, I envision a dashboard type contraption near the handlebars that will hold a cell phone, GPS, computer, and more. I want to make sure that you each have the best of everything so you're never out of communication with each other or your mother and I, and that you never get lost on our property. OK?" Clem asked.

"Sounds like a plan, Dad," Braun said. "Oh, one other thing, Dad, how are you going to handle my big tail? Will that be a problem?"

"I think I've figured it out, Braun," Clem responded, unrolling a huge piece of white paper with a sketch of a motorcycle on it. "Here, come here and take a look."

Braun moved closer and looked down at the sketch Clem held in his hands.

"Ah, beautiful. That's BONE-A-FIDE!"

With their interest peaked by Braun's enthusiasm, the four other dinosaurs moved closer to see the drawing themselves. Clem had sketched a huge motorcycle with a sidecar for Braun's tail. The sketch even showed how his tail would coil up in the sidecar so that it stayed out of the way while he was riding.

"That's pretty ingenious, Dad," Trex said.

Clem nodded, accepting the compliment. "Thanks, Trex."

"Well, if we get started first thing tomorrow morning, we ought to have all five motorcycles built in about two months.

That is, if you all help out. Are you willing to do that?" Clem asked.

"Absolutely," they all said at the same time.

"OK. Then let's meet in my workshop tomorrow at 8:00 a.m. sharp to go over what each of you want your bike to look like. That will give you time to think about it tonight. Once we know the full scope of what we have to build, we can get started. Sound like a plan?" Clem asked.

"Sounds like a plan, Dad. See you at 8:00 a.m. on the dot," Braun said.

"Well, I'll be there as close to 8:00 as possible. I have to get my beauty sleep, you know," Riz said.

"Why? It doesn't seem to be working," laughed Trex.

"You be quiet, Mr. Magic Stick Man," Riz shot back.

"No more of that, you two," Joan said. "Meet your father at 8:00 a.m. sharp as he's asked you to. Now, hurry, get to bed."

www.thefossibles.com

CHAPTER 11

Bummer Summer Day

It was just about 8:30 the next morning when the five dinosaurs finally assembled in Clem's workshop. Deb and Trex each brought along their own sketches.

"Before we start, let's remember that I run a real business here. I have customers in and out of here all day long. None of them can see any of you or you could all be in danger. Understand?" Clem asked.

"Understand, Dad," Trex responded for the group.

"OK, then we all must keep our eyes and ears open all the time. If anyone hears anything or sees dust rising from the driveway because a car or motorcycle is driving toward the house, yell out to me right away. When that happens, all of you must drop whatever you're doing and run out the back door and get over to the Bone Zone as quickly as you can. No lollygagging. No questioning. I'd rather be safe than sorry. I'll let you know when it's safe to come back. OK?"

"OK, Dad," Deb said.

"That's easy for you to say, Deb. You run so fast, no one could ever spot you," said Riz.

"For crying out loud, Riz, just put it in gear and run to the Bone Zone. I've seen you move when you have to. And, in this situation, you have to," Deb countered.

"Can I just run into the house and stay with Mom?" Little T asked.

"Of course you can, Little T. But, the rest of you must get back to the Bone Zone. Now, let's get started on building these bikes," Clem said excitedly. "Who wants to go first and tell me what you want?"

"I will, Dad," Trex said, handing Clem his rough drawing. Clem examined the big, sturdy design with a place to hold his magic stick and nodded approval. Then, he looked at the design Deb had drawn, a bike with a very sleek, turbo look to it. "OK. These are definitely doable. You all saw the design of Braun's last night, the one with the sidecar. What about you, Riz? What do you want?"

"I don't have a sketch of it, Dad, but I want it to really fit my body so it's easy for me to drive and I want it to have big flowers for exhaust pipes."

"I'm assuming each of you will paint your own bike once it's built so you can put flowers on it wherever you want, Riz," Clem responded.

"That's not what I'm talking about. I want the actual exhaust pipes to be shaped like beautiful flowers. Is that possible?"

"For you, Riz, anything's possible," Clem said, winking at her. "OK, last but not least, Little T. What do you want?"

"I want a jazzy red bike that goes fast and is low to the ground," Little T said emphatically.

"A jazzy red bike that goes fast it is. Well, maybe not all that fast," Clem replied. And, as quick as that, work began on building all five motorcycles.

One hot summer day, the dinosaurs were forced to quickly run out of their father's repair shop just like they'd been instructed to do by their parents before the work began on the motorcycles. It all started when Trex thought he heard a loud, sputtering motor and looked out the window to check. Sure enough, a big mustard yellow tank-like SUV was hobbling up the driveway with its' motor coughing all the way. Dust swirled up from the dirt driveway and enveloped the vehicle as it rumbled along.

"Hurry! Get to the Bone Zone! Someone's coming!" Trex yelled. The four older dinosaurs immediately dropped what they were doing and darted out the back door towards the Bone Zone. As previously agreed, Little T ran to the safety of his parents' home. The back doors of Clem's shop slammed shut an instant before the front door opened to reveal a disheveled, wide-eyed man.

"Hello. What can I help you with?" asked Clem.

"My SUV's acting up. Can you take a look?"

"Sure."

Both men moved outside into the glaring mid-day Arizona sun.

"My name's Clem Stone. What's yours?" Clem asked while extending his hand.

"Dr. Dimitri Roy. I'm a paleontologist working on a dinosaur dig west of here. Just went into Phoenix to pick up supplies and the mail. It's hard to get anyone to drive out to the location of our dig. Too remote."

"Dinosaurs? I didn't know they ever existed in Arizona." Suddenly, Clem was very uneasy. He shot a glance over Dr. Roy's shoulders toward the Bone Zone, hopeful that none of his kids were visible. He quickened his pace to fix Dr. Roy's vehicle so he'd get on his way as soon as possible.

"Oh, yes. This area was heavily populated with various dinosaur species millions and millions of years ago. Some areas around here are the richest bone beds in the United States."

"Gee, I didn't know that. Very interesting. There you go. It's all fixed. Minor problem. It's just a loose bolt. See here. This is where I tightened it."

Dr. Roy leaned his head into the engine compartment to see what Clem was pointing at.

"Thanks. What do I owe you?"

"It's nothing, nothing at all. Glad to be able to help you out. Good luck with that dig," Clem said, anxious to move the good doctor along on his journey and get him away from his kids.

"Thank you, again. Good bye."

Dr. Roy hopped into the driver's seat of his vehicle. He turned it around and began to drive down the driveway. Suddenly, his eyes scanned the Bone Zone and he stopped abruptly. Rolling down the window, he yelled to Clem. "Hey, what's that big building over there? Do you repair airplanes too?"

"No. It's a place where we have events and exhibitions for folks in the area. It's on my property because all my neighbors respect the fact I'll take care of it. Plus, I can fix anything."

"I know you can. I appreciate your help. Good bye again."

With that, Dr. Roy drove down the long driveway to the main road and headed west.

Clem watched him all the way, anxious to make sure that he did, in fact, leave.

As he watched the bright mustard yellow SUV disappear into the western horizon, he slumped down against his pickup truck.

Joan appeared from the house. Apparently she'd been monitoring the actions of their visitor too.

"Who was he? What did he want?"

"You're not going to believe this, Joan. He's a paleontologist and he's on a dinosaur dig west of here."

"What?"

"That's right. A dinosaur dig. Thank goodness our kids stayed out of sight."

"Thank goodness is right."

And, as Dr. Roy drove away, he sensed a peculiar connection to Clem Stone and the property he'd just visited. Unsure of why he felt such a connection, he shrugged it off and continued back to the dig. Like most of his other digs, this one wasn't going that well either. Consequently, he had some ranting and raving to do. Slowly, his bird rose up out of the front passenger seat and looked back at Clem Stone's property as it disappeared from view.

CHAPTER 12

Five Equal One

As the work on building the motorcycles continued, the dinosaurs expressed an overwhelming concern to Clem. Yes, they each desperately wanted a motorcycle. But they didn't want the motorcycles fueled by fossil fuel. Anything but that! Could Clem invent an alternative fuel, they asked.

Clem was immediately sympathetic to their feelings and beliefs. So, work stopped on all the bikes as he experimented with different types of fuels of his own creation. Soon, his workshop was littered with numerous odd-colored liquids in glass decanters. Clem tested the contents of each several times. He jotted down numbers on a big yellow pad, held the decanters to the light, tested the efficiency of each fuel in a skeletal bike he kept in the shop, and repeatedly grunted indicating success or failure.

At last, he gathered all five dinosaurs together in his workshop and proclaimed, "I've figured it out. Don't ask me how. Don't ask me why. But, we'll fuel your motorcycles with cactus juice."

"Cactus juice!" yelled Riz. "How'd you figure that out?"

"That's what I've been doing all my life, Riz- figuring things out. This is a great solution. I've harvested the juice from cacti on our own property. The good news is that there's a lot more where this came from. We can fuel your bikes for years to come."

"Great, Dad. We're so proud of you."

"I second that, Dad. You're remarkable."

"Thanks, Braun."

And so, from that point, one by one, the motorcycles were engineered to be powered by cactus juice.

Then, each dinosaur painted their own bike. In the end, no two were alike. Each reflected the personality of the dinosaur who would drive it.

Little T got just what he asked for-a bright red bike that was low to the ground. Riz got her exhaust pipes shaped like big flowers with long stems. Then, she painted the entire bike in multi-colored flowers-green, pink, blue, red, yellow, and orange. Trex painted his bike deep blue and put flames on the chassis. Deb's was fast and sleek, just like her. She painted it orange and yellow, her favorite colors. And, as for the big bike with the sidecar, Braun painted it all shiny silver.

Finally, the big day arrived. Almost exactly two months to the day after work had begun, all the motorcycles were finished. Joan and Clem helped the dinosaurs roll their bikes out into the sun. Each quickly jumped on, anxious to start their bikes and go riding.

Rumpf!, Rumpf! Rumpf! Braun had ignition. Joan covered her ears, as the other four bikes were started.

"Clem, they're so loud. Someone will hear," she yelled, still covering her ears.

"Don't worry, Joan. They'll just assume I'm working on some very loud bikes."

"BONE-A-FIDE," Braun tried to yell over the sound of his engine. He smiled broadly, loving the sound. Rumpf! Rumpf! The noise kept getting louder as he played with the throttle.

"Now, remember what I told you. Ride only on our property. Do not go off of it. Go slow at first and stay together. Remember to help each other out if anyone needs help. You hear me?" Clem shouted.

The dinosaurs nodded, each chomping at the bit to take off and ride. They put their helmets on and waited for Clem to give them a thumb's up. All revved their engines and the noise was deafening.

"OK, give it a whirl. Let's see how these things really work," Clem yelled as he gave the thumbs up sign. "Be back in a half hour."

And, with that simple directive, all five dinosaurs took off riding their new motorcycles. Clem and Joan watched as they rode off in a group, remaining in view of their parents. All, including Little T, did a fine job riding. Each had remarkable balance and, because they thoroughly understood the mechanics of their bikes, knew how to get them to perform at ultimate capacity.

As Joan and Clem watched their five kids ride off for the first time, both realized that each of the dinosaurs had defied amazing odds to get to where they were today. In the process, they'd taught Joan and Clem that anything's possible.

"They're remarkable, Joan. Don't you think so?" Clem asked, shaking his head in amazement.

"Absolutely. They're so special and I love them so much. I'm really glad we decided to keep them all to ourselves when they were born. Aren't you, Clem?"

"Without a doubt! They have such a great, positive spirit. It's definitely contagious. When we were building the bikes, I had a perfect opportunity to spend lots of time with them, with all of them together. They're the best at helping each other out. Oh sure, they joke with each other all the time, just like most brothers and sisters do. But, when push comes to shove, Joan, they're there for each other. Guess we have ourselves to thank for that," Clem said.

"Maybe so. But, something else seems to drive them. I'm not exactly sure what it is, but there's something there. I just can't put my finger on it."

"Well, wait 'til they get back here. I've got a surprise for them and you. It's something I've been thinking about for a while now," Clem said.

"What is it?" Joan asked.

"Wait and see."

As instructed, in a half hour, the dinosaurs returned, each bubbling with excitement.

"Wow! That was fuuuuuunnnnnnnn!" Little T exclaimed.

"You think so, Little Guy?" Trex asked, patting Little T on the back. "I think it was more than a little fun. I know what I'm going to be doing from now on, that's for sure."

"I'm really out of breath," Riz huffed. "I've got to learn to shut my mouth when I'm riding. I just ate a lot of yucky bugs. UGH!"

"Now, that's a stretch for you, Riz. Keeping your mouth shut," Deb heckled.

Riz ignored her.

"My tail fits in the sidecar so well, Dad. What a great idea," Braun said.

"I'm glad, Braun. I knew we'd find something you could drive. Didn't I tell you that awhile back?" Joan asked.

"Yeah, you did, Mom."

Clem cleared his throat and said, "I've got something to say and I'd like all of you to pay attention." He continued. "For a long time now, your mother and I have watched you grow. Individually, each of you is very special. And, together, the five of you are one pretty remarkable team. I don't think there's anything you won't be able to accomplish in life. It's amazing how far each of you has come from those five eggs buried deep in that cave."

He hesitated a moment and then said, "Consequently, from now on, when we're referring to the five of you, we're going to call you the Fossibles, a word I coined to honor both your dinosaur heritage and your prevailing spirit of possibility. How does that sound?"

"Fossibles. Fossibles," Deb said the word slowly, letting it sink in. "I like it, Dad."

"Me too," Trex replied.

"I'd say that Fossibles is BONE-A-FIDE!" Braun said signifying his approval.

"Oh, you mean, from now on anything's fossible," Riz joked as she played on the word her father had just said. And then she burst into song in her most annoying, fake theater voice, "Anything's fossible, fossible, fossible! Anything's fossible!"

"Riz, actually that's pretty good, that is, as long as you don't try to sing it," Joan laughed. "Really though, with the five of you, anything is fossible! You've always lived your lives with that belief and Dad and I want you to continue doing so throughout your lives. Do you hear what we're saying?"

"We do, Mom. We do," Braun said.

"Me too," Little T piped in so as not to be ignored. "I understand. We're the Fossibles and anything's fossible!"

"Good job, Little T. You've got it," Clem said approvingly. Turning to all of them, he continued, "Now, Fossibles, let's get these bikes inside, clean them off, and then go over to the Bone Zone and chow down."

Trex interrupted, "One more thing. You know what? From now on, I think I'll call my magic stick the Fossilizer. Doesn't that sound cool?"

"Whatever, Trex. Fossilizer, magic stick, it's pretty much all the same. Just seems like a silly stick that you're way too attached to if you ask me," Riz said.

"Oh, yeah, Riz? Well, you'll see. The Fossilizer is more than a stick. Way more," Trex responded emphatically.

"Now that's enough bickering you two," Clem said. "Let's go in and have dinner. And, while you're at it, Trex, bring your Fossilizer with you," Clem said smiling and giving a thumbs up to Trex.

Chapter 13

Curiosi-T

From the day they first drove their new motorcycles, the Fossibles had something very special that they all loved to do—ride. So as not to be seen, they usually rode their bikes at night. Over time, they developed a good understanding of what made up the seventy-five acres on which their family lived. From the rocky western border to the prairie-like eastern border, the Fossibles explored and learned all they could. During their rides, each continued to dream about actually becoming part of the human race and being able to play games and hang out with other kids. But, they kept their dreams to themselves and didn't mention anything to their Mom and Dad. Why make them worry?

During daylight hours, the Fossibles followed pretty much the same routine. After school and homework, they all had their chores to do and they all had to help their parents. In the afternoon, they split up and did things on their own. Little T would skateboard. Deb would practice yoga and karate. Trex would email and chat online. Riz would produce her own TV show in her bedroom. Braun would tinker with the bikes in the garage.

Even though their daily routines sometimes seemed humdrum, they all knew they were not allowed to expand their horizons and leave their parents' property. Joan and Clem remained adamant about them not being seen by humans. They couldn't risk what might happen if they were discovered so they made sure the Fossibles knew they meant it.

"Mom, can I please go into town with you? Please?" Riz begged.

"No, absolutely not, Riz. I've told you before. It's too dangerous. Now, just tell me what you need and I'll pick it up for you," replied Joan.

"But I can hide in the back of the pick-up underneath a blanket or something. No one will see me. I promise. I don't understand. I just want to see a mall and a grocery store and people for that matter. I mean, do they dress nice or would I be giving fashion citations out everywhere?" Riz continued.

"You can't go. Don't you ever listen to Mom?" asked Trex.

"I would love to go myself. I would just like to see people or go to the college and watch all of the kids running around," Deb remarked.

"None of you are going anywhere and I mean it. Please, take it from me. No one would understand and you could get very, very hurt and that, well, that would be the end of me for sure.

Now, Riz, what do you want me to get for you in town?" Joan snapped.

"I don't know, maybe some new fabric for another coat, maybe with flowers or stripes. Stripes, yeah, stripes," Riz said, and obediently, but glumly, walked off toward the Bone Zone.

Deb shrugged her shoulders, hugged her mother and followed Riz. Trex stood there and gave Joan a look as if to say "Don't worry I'll keep an eye on them." Joan smiled and headed toward the truck. Little T was riding his board back and forth on the half pipe when Joan drove by and waved. Little T shot up his arm to wave back.

The days all seemed to blend together for the Fossibles, one into the other. That is, until one day their lives changed forever.

Little T was bored. After many failed attempts to get his brothers and sisters to play with him, he was left to his own devices. He got on his motorcycle and started to ride around the property. Off in the distance, he heard something. It sounded like cheers. But, it was hard to tell. Then, he heard it again. It sounded like people having fun at a game or something. He looked around and saw that no one was outside. He thought this was his big chance and, in a split second, he totally disregarded his parents' rules and rode off toward the main road.

As he raced down the road wearing his fighter pilot helmet, Little T's heart beat a mile a minute. He wasn't nervous, just excited. The world looked wonderful out here. Why were his parents so adamant about him not leaving their property? He couldn't understand.

Soon, he came upon a red sign with eight sides and it said STOP. He put on the breaks and stopped. Then, he looked around and saw that there was no one there. He wondered why there was a sign telling you to STOP when no one else was around. He waited for awhile and still nothing happened. "NOW WHAT?" Little T yelled loudly. Nobody answered him, so he started off again, racing down the street.

Finally, he came upon a school with a baseball field right along the road. Little T slowed down. A real baseball game was in progress. He stopped his motorcycle behind a big bush and got off.

Back at the house, Clem and Braun walked out of the garage toward the half pipe. "Have you seen Little T?" asked Clem, looking around.

"No, not since lunch. He's probably out on his bike somewhere," answered Braun.

Little T got off his bike and stood near the fence. There were a lot of trees and shrubs. He slowly pushed his bike into the brush so as not to be seen. As he peaked through the brush, he was amazed at what he saw. A real Little League game was in full swing. All of the kids had great colorful outfits, real baseball equipment, and lots of cheering fans in the bleachers. Little T thought it was awesome.

As he watched the next hitter get up to bat, he became so entranced with the game that he didn't realize he had become too comfortable leaning against the fence and was no longer hiding from the crowd. Suddenly, a loud cry was heard, "WHAT'S THHHAAATTTT?"

In a split second, Little T realized the cry was about him. Someone had spotted him. He looked toward the baseball field and saw people pointing and heard them shouting at him. Some of the men started to run toward him. "Call the police" could be heard followed by "Hurry, don't let it get away!"

Little T got very scared and frantically tried to put his helmet back on. He knew he needed to get on his bike and get out of there as quickly as he could. Just then, an arm reached out and clubbed him in the side of the stomach. It hurt and his instinct told him to hit back. So, he started swinging. All these big, strong people were yelling and trying to tackle him.

"WHAT IS IT?" a man yelled as he tried to wrestle Little T to the ground.

"LET GO OF ME," Little T shrieked.

"He TALKS," another man yelled incredulously. "Grab his legs and hold down his arms," he ordered.

Little T struggled and felt like he was fighting for his life. He wanted his brothers and sisters to come and save him. He longed to be back in the safety of the Bone Zone.

All of a sudden, flashbulbs started to go off. One of the spectators at the game had called the police and, now, even the news stations were en route. Everybody gathered in a semi-circle around the spot where Little T lay. Moms blocked their kids' eyes and hugged them tightly. Some people ran off to the safety of their cars. Police carrying clubs ran into the circle to apprehend the monster.

Little T kept struggling and fighting back. Someone had ripped his coat. The men were trying to hold him down on the ground. Suddenly, Little T used his power to camouflage himself and instantly turned the color of the ground, fading from sight.

"Where'd he go?" asked one confused officer.

"I don't know, but I can feel him. He's still fighting," responded another officer.

Back at the house, Joan was just finishing up the lunch dishes when she heard the local news interrupted by the announcer saying he had breaking news to report.

"Now, let's go live to Camden Fields just outside Phoenix where local police are trying to apprehend what appears to be a giant lizard, a lizard that's wearing clothes just like a human being. A lizard that police say can speak English," said the announcer. "Bryant, can you tell us what's going on?"

Joan moved slowly toward the TV and, as the picture came on, her heart sank. There was Little T's bike leaned up against the bushes. "MY BABY," she yelled. She ran outside and kept yelling, "MY BABY, MY BABY." Quickly, her yells turned to cries. Clem, Braun, Riz, Trex, and Deb ran up to her immediately.

"TV, TV, TV, go look at the TV," Joan stuttered. She could barely talk as tears streamed down her cheeks. Clem and Deb ran quickly into the living room while Braun, Trex, and Riz stayed at their mother's side comforting her.

"NOOOOOOOOOOOOOOOOO," screamed Clem and then he and Deb ran back outside.

"Get your motorcycles, quick. Follow me. We have to hurry. Little T has been seen by people and now the police are trying to apprehend him, right now, right this minute. He needs our help. Quick, move," Clem ordered, as he ran toward his truck.

Trex, Riz, Braun, and Deb immediately ran to their bikes, started them up, and put on their helmets. They all looked at each other and somehow, without saying a word, knew that this would be the end of life as they had known it. Trex clutched the Fossilizer tightly, whispered something to it, and then attached it to the holder near his handlebars.

Clem pulled his truck up next to Joan and rolled down the window. "Don't worry. We'll bring our baby back. I love you," he said and drove off. Trex, Riz, Braun, and Deb followed the truck. Joan stood there until she could no longer see the truck or the bikes and then went back into the house to watch her whole life unfold very publicly on TV.

As Clem drove up to Camden Fields, he saw a very large crowd of people. The Fossibles were right behind his truck, but no one paid any attention to them. News stations had already set up satellite dishes and were broadcasting live from the scene. Police, helicopters, news reporters, and frightened adults were everywhere. It was mass hysteria.

Clem slowed down to take a look. He could see the spot where Little T was struggling and he could see his bike propped against the bush. Clem waved Deb on to come up close to the window of his truck. "Deb, it's time you use your screeching power. Give me one good one, and make it loud," Clem said.

Deb put her feet down to steady herself on her bike and took off her helmet. Leaning her head back, her bone touched the back of her neck and, all of a sudden, she shot off her highest pitched screech. Glass started shattering on all the cars and trucks, even Clem's. The big camera lights started breaking. All the people grabbed their ears. "Keep it up, Deb, it's working," yelled Clem holding his own ears.

Little T heard Deb's familiar screeching noise and knew his family was close by. In a blink of an eye, the policemen let go of him so they could grab their own ears. And, when they released their grip, Little T jumped up and ran over and grabbed his bike. He jumped on and rode toward where the noise was coming from. He got excited when he saw his Dad and all of his brothers and sisters waving him on. Just as he reached them, Deb stopped making her noise.

"Come on. Let's go. We have to move fast," yelled Clem. He looked around and saw that everyone now realized that Little T was escaping, a realization that came just as their hearing started to come back. Deb put her helmet back on and began to kick start her bike. But, the police had already made a blockade around the Fossibles and Clem. Everyone stared in amazement at these five lizard-like creatures in human cloth-ing that were driving souped-up motorcycles. The police had their guns drawn. "Don't move," shouted one of the officers. Clem put his truck in park and opened the door.

"I can explain," he said as he stepped out of the truck. "Stop. Don't move. Stay right where you are. You'll have a lot of time to explain," commanded an officer with his gun pointed right at Braun. Just then a huge police truck pulled up. The driver looked shocked when he saw what he was about to transport.

Kids, sympathetic to the Fossibles, cried out, "Don't hurt them! Don't hurt them!"

Onlookers were stunned. What were these creatures who stood in front of them, gigantic lizards dressed like humans? An eerie silence fell over the crowd. The only noise that could be heard was that of reporters talking quietly into their microphones.

"Do what they say, "Clem instructed his kids softly. "It will be okay. I promise."

"I'm scared," squealed Riz.

"Who just said that?" asked the astonished chief of police, Paul McWill. He looked around and knew he was going to need more back-up.

"I WANT ALL OF YOU TO TURN AROUND AND PLACE YOUR ARMS BEHIND YOUR HEADS," instructed Chief McWill in a very loud voice.

The Fossibles and Clem did as they were told. You could hear a pin drop. No one moved. Slowly, they put their hands on their heads. The police moved in closer and closer. Then, one officer grabbed Clem. After all, he was human so the officer knew what he was dealing with. As several officers approached each one of the Fossibles, it became quite clear to them that, whatever these creatures were, they were as frightened as the police were.

"The cuffs don't fit," yelled officer Hasson. "Their arms are too big. What do we do?"

"What are you?" asked an officer speaking directly into Deb's ear.

"We are dinosaurs, sir, and we mean you no harm. My brother left the house by accident today. We just want to go home," explained Deb softly.

"DINOSAURS!!!!!!" exclaimed the officer loudly. "Hey, Chief, they're dinosaurs!"

All the kids in the crowd began to smile. This was nothing like they'd ever seen before. They'd only read about dinosaurs. And, dinosaurs weren't supposed to be alive anymore. They'd vanished from the planet millions and millions of years ago. Kids yelled with excitement and the noise from the crowd swelled. All watched in amazement as the Fossibles and Clem were loaded into the back of the police truck.

"What about our motorcycles?" Trex asked before he stepped up into the police truck. "Where are you taking them?"

"Don't worry. We're putting them into that other truck right over there," Chief McWill said, pointing to a huge truck parked on the road behind them. "It'll follow us to the police station."

"Can I get something off my bike before we go?" Trex asked, concerned about the Fossilizer.

"What?" Chief McWill asked.

"That stick attached to my handle bars. See it? I don't like to go anywhere without it," Trex answered.

"No, definitely not. It looks like a weapon to me. Now, go ahead, get into the truck like I asked you to."

Slowly Trex turned and reluctantly entered the police truck. From inside, he looked out toward his motorcycle to make sure the Fossilizer was still there. He caught a glimpse of it hanging from his bike and, right then, Chief McWill slammed the doors of the truck shut. Slowly, the truck drove away surrounded by about thirty police cars, all with their sirens blaring and their lights flashing.

Back at home, Joan sat on the couch, and watched the scene unfold on TV. She gasped when she saw her entire family led into the back of the police truck. She could tell from the expressions on their faces, the Fossibles were frightened, very frightened. She put her face into her hands and started to cry.

CHAPTER 14

Power[5]

The ride in the back of the police truck was bumpy. Except for a few rays of bright light that shone in around the vertical bars on the back windows, it was very dark. Clem sat in the back of the truck. His mind raced as he looked at his five children. Each one had a look of terror on their face and they all sat very still. No one said a word until Braun spoke, almost in a whisper.

"Dad, with my strength, I bet I could break through these doors and we could all escape," Braun said.

"I could charge them," Riz piped up as she looked toward the front of the truck to make sure the driver didn't hear her.

"No, kids. That would only make matters worse. We've got to face whatever it is we're up against. Please remember everything your mother and I have taught you. I don't know how this will turn out, but promise me you will all behave with the utmost respect and do exactly what they tell you to do," Clem said solemnly, looking over at Little T. Little T put his head down resting his chin on his chest and took a deep breath.

"I am so sorry, Dad. I am so sorry. It's all my fault. What's going to happen to us? Where are they taking us? I am so, so scared," Little T whimpered and began to cry. He leaned his head on Deb's shoulder. She tried to comfort him by moving closer and holding him tight. She looked over at her father.

Clem knew exactly where the police station was, yet today's ride seemed unusually long. His mind began to drift back to various times in his life — living in Massachusetts, being a professor, his move to Arizona, finding the dinosaur eggs, his kids' births, all the good times, all the bad times, building the Bone Zone, the Fossibles' first bike rides, and much, much more. He and Joan had created a real family. Now, the pit in the bottom of his stomach told him that all this might be coming to an end. Just then, his thoughts were abruptly interrupted as the truck stopped at a traffic light and sirens blared from all directions. "Now what?" Clem thought. The driver's radio went off, but it was hard to understand what was being said.

"All county vehicles, please be advised, help is needed immediately at the intersection of Main and Brayer. I repeat, all officers, report to Main and Brayer, code 512, code 512." The female dispatcher's voice sounded raspy and, although the signal kept breaking up, portions of what she was saying were audible. The driver of the police truck picked up his CB radio and called in.

"This is truck 918HN," the driver said. "I have the lizards, or whatever they are, in the back of my truck. Should I divert to respond to the call at Main and Brayer?" The woman's voice came back on and said "I repeat, all police and fire vehicles head to Main and Brayer. I repeat, all police and fire vehicles report..." The driver just shook his head and took a sharp left turn heading for the intersection of Main and Brayer, muttering under his breath, "That's easy for you to say!"

When the truck finally came to a stop, the driver got out to talk to the officer in charge. The Fossibles and Clem could hear loud yelling and screaming. Braun slowly moved his long neck and head to the window in the back of the truck so he could look out and see what was going on.

"What do you see, Braun?" Clem asked.

"Dad, a big building is on fire. I see people trapped on the roof and the firemen are having a hard time reaching them because their ladders are just too short," Braun said.

"Dad, we have to go out there and help," shouted Trex. "Please, let's break out of this truck and help them. The police will understand. Won't they?"

Clem thought for a moment and then answered, "Go ahead. Just do it. Hurry up and help those people."

In a split second, Braun busted out of his chains as did Trex and Little T. They helped undo Deb and Riz. Then, Braun and Trex quickly pushed the back doors of the truck open, breaking the outside locks and letting sunlight pour in. Everyone, including Clem, had to take a moment to let their eyes adjust to the blinding glare. Then, the Fossibles jumped out of the back of the police truck.

People were running around everywhere and the building was now completely engulfed in big, hot red flames. The acrid smell of the burning building permeated the air. The ladders from the fire trucks were too short to reach to the top floors or to the roof of the building. In one window, a mother and her young son frantically waved their arms, pleading to be rescued. Thick, black smoke billowed into the late afternoon air as more people could be seen on the roof and in other upper windows signaling for help.

Braun immediately swung into action. He yelled for Little T to get into position. Little T jumped onto the end of Braun's tail and held on tight. With one giant swoop, Braun catapulted Little T upward toward the mother and son who were yelling for help in one of the upper windows. For a split second the firemen, police, and onlookers watched in amazement as Little T flew through the sky right past them. He landed on the side of the building and quickly grabbed the window frame where the mother and son were.

"You're going to be fine. Just hold on," Little T said as he looked into the mother's eyes that were filled with both worry and curiosity at the same time. Braun jumped on top of the fire truck and extended his tail up as high as he could toward Little T. As soon as the tail reached Little T, he grabbed it and instructed the mother and son, "I want you to climb out, hold onto me, and slide down my brother's tail," Little T said. The wind had changed and the flames and smoke were so bad that the people on the ground could no longer see what was actually happening near the top of the building.

"I can't do it. I'm scared. I just can't," cried the mother. "My son will die. No, I can't do it. No!" As she was speaking, a huge crash thundered through the smoky air as a major chunk of the building collapsed.

"Hear that? We don't have much time. You can do this. You must," Little T yelled. "Now let me have him. I promise he will be fine. Let's go."

The mother handed Little T her son's arm, as if to say, "Okay, he is in your hands now." Little T looked at the boy. He was having difficulty breathing and was choking badly on the heavy, putrid smoke.

"Okay, all you have to do is hold on and slide down my brother's tail. Think of it as a slide at school, okay?" Little T said to the boy. The boy reached up and grabbed onto Little T who helped him out the window and placed him on Braun's tail. The boy started to cry. The height frightened him and, because of the intense smoke, his bearings were off. All of a sudden, the boy straddled Braun's tail and, without saying another word, slid down the tail and out of sight. His mother screamed in anguish as he disappeared into the thick blanket of smoke.

"He's fine, he's fine. Now, it's your turn," yelled Little T as he shot out his arm to help her climb out the window. At this point, Little T actually had no idea whether or not the little boy was fine because he couldn't see the ground either. Slowly, the mother climbed out the window and steadied herself by leaning on Little T. She then climbed onto Braun's tail and, looking up at Little T, said, "Thank you, whatever you are. Thank you." She began to sob. Little T nodded his head, smiled at her and, without saying another word, she too slid out of sight.

When the mother landed on Braun's back, a fireman grabbed her, helped her off and quickly covered her with a blanket. Then, he applied an oxygen mask to her face. Turning, she saw her son lying on an ambulance stretcher next to her and she sobbed big tears of relief. Little T came zipping down Braun's tail and jumped off. He looked at Braun and winked.

"Thank you. Thank you so much. You saved our lives. How will I ever repay you?" the mother asked.

"No need to repay us. We were glad to help," Braun said.

Riz charged over to a nearby stream where the firemen were getting water for their pumper truck. She knelt down and began inhaling water. She inhaled so much water that she quickly blew up like a hot air balloon. Once she was filled to capacity, she turned around and headed back toward the building. As she walked, she looked like a giant balloon floating slowly toward the fire. As she reached the side of the building, she began to expel water in large quantities right onto the burning fire. Firemen and police could not believe what a force she was. Quickly, the flames around Riz extinguished. She continued inhaling and exhaling gallons of water to help put out the fire.

The firemen were having big problems with their ladders. None reached high enough to help save the people standing on the roof. But Braun knew what to do. He used his incredible strength to pick one of the fire trucks up off the ground and extended it as high as he could into the air over his head. Then, Deb bolted up the extended ladder that now easily reached all the people in distress. She expertly guided them down to safety. While all this was going on, Trex continuously jumped from the ground directly onto the roof top and brought people down to safety two at a time.

Onlookers watched in amazement as this team of five dinosaurs took control of the situation and rescued all the people. It became clear that they were not an evil threat. Instead, they were heroes, real heroes. But, who were they? Where had they come from?

Clem, still handcuffed, sat in the back of the police truck with the doors swung open, and watched as his five children performed like the super heroes he'd always known they were. He was so very proud of them. And, now other people were learning the truth about the Fossibles, a truth that he and Joan had known for a long, long time.

Now that the fire was under control, people started to gather around Deb, Riz, Trex, Little T, and Braun. One of the officers removed Clem's handcuffs and brought him over to his children. Quickly, he gave each a long, lingering hug.

The townspeople, police, firemen, and local officials were all stunned by the Fossibles' heroism and superpowers. The media that had only moments earlier filmed their capture, were now broadcasting the Fossibles' amazing feats live to every corner of the world. As the circle of curiosity seekers widened around the dinosaurs, cameras were pointed directly at them and huge microphones were stuck in their faces. The questions seemed never ending for both the Fossibles and Clem.

"Where did you find them, Mr. Stone?"

"How did you all learn to speak English?"

"When did you know they were dinosaurs?"

"How long have they been living with you?"

"Where did you get those powers?"

"Who built your motorcycles?"

"Why do you call yourselves the Fossibles?"

Questions streamed non-stop from the crowd. But it was obvious that the tone of the crowd had changed. They no longer thought the dinosaurs were monsters. Instead, they had seen first hand that these dinosaurs had human-like qualities and possessed superpowers that were far greater than those of anyone else on earth.

Finally, after enduring about an hour of direct questions, Clem spoke to the crowd with the Chief of Police at his side. "If you don't mind, I would like to stop the questioning for now and take my kids, the Fossibles, home where I am sure my wife, Joan, is worried sick," Clem said, looking at Chief McWill to verify that he could, in fact, do that. "We would be happy to accommodate any questions or interviews anyone has at a later date, say tomorrow after we all get a good night's rest," Clem continued.

Chief McWill piped up. "Mr. Stone, they just patched in a call from the President of the United States who has told me that for now, you are all free to go home. The White House will be contacting you soon for information regarding your dinosaurs, excuse me, I mean your children." The Chief winked at Clem who looked out at the crowd that had gathered and then at his five kids. Little T was already signing autographs for some of the kids and Riz was talking to some girl about the flowered pants she was wearing. They were each so engulfed by all the attention they were getting. Clem watched for a moment and then said, "Okay, guys, it's time to head home. I hate to break up this party, but let's get going. Your mother's waiting for us."

Trex, Riz, Braun, Deb, and Little T all got on their motorcycles and revved their engines. Clem jumped into his battered pick-up truck and shut the door. Chief McWill walked up to the driver's side of the car to speak with him. Clem didn't need to roll down the window because Deb had blown out all the glass on his truck with her screeches earlier in the day. Glass shards were all over the floor of the truck and around the rim of the window.

"Mr. Stone, I think it would be best if we give you a police escort home. We wouldn't want anything to happen to any of you, now would we?"

Clem laughed and so did Chief McWill as he motioned six police cruisers into formation ahead of Clem and the Fossibles. The officers put on their sirens and lights and the crowd slowly moved back to let their new heroes pass. People yelled and cheered as Clem and the five very unique creatures slowly followed each other away from the scene of the fire. Trex gingerly clasped the Fossilizer close to his chest just to keep it safe. As they drove away, the crowd began to chant, "anything's fossible!"

Back at home, Joan still sat in the same place on the couch, eyes fixed on the TV. She'd been there all day. She saw her family head for home and started to cry again. But, this time it wasn't for fear of her children being taken to prison. No, this time it was for fear of the outside world, the new demands that would be placed on the Fossibles, the phone calls, and then, it happened ... ring, ring, ring! Let the games begin!

www.thefossibles.com

CHAPTER 15

Am I Dreaming?

Dr. Roy was attending an important scientific conference in London where he was to give a speech on vertebrate paleontology and major happenings throughout the world. Because of the time change, it was much later in the day in London than it was in Arizona.

In fact, at the time the Fossibles were being discovered at the baseball field, Dr. Roy was in bed. Actually, he was sleeping pretty soundly because he always left all the lights on in his hotel room to counter his fear of the dark. Suddenly, the phone on his night stand rang. He answered. A fellow paleontologist was on the line.

"Dimitri, do you have TV on?"

"No. I'm sleeping. What's going on?"

"Turn on the news channel. Turn it on right now. You're not going to believe this!"

Dr. Roy picked up the remote and hit the power button. He scrolled down to the news channel and, once the image focused, he couldn't believe his eyes.

"From Camden Fields outside of Phoenix, Arizona, this is Hugh Mubley bringing you breaking news of something none of us ever thought we'd see. Apparently, a discovery of five live dinosaurs has just been made. These dinosaurs act like human kids yet look like their dinosaur ancestors. They ride souped-up motorcycles. Local law enforcement has taken them into custody, unsure of what's really going on. We'll continue to cover this live. Right now it looks like they've all been rounded up at a baseball game here at Camden Fields."

Dr. Roy squinted at the TV screen. Yes, they did look like dinosaurs. But, could this be? The camera panned the group of dinosaurs as they were being put into the back of a police truck for transportation to the station. Dr. Roy thought he recognized the man that was accompanying them. He looked closer. He was sure it was the guy who'd fixed his SUV a few months back while he was on a dig in Arizona.

"Yes, I'm sure that's him," he mumbled to himself.

As news cameras followed the police truck on its' trip to the station, they captured the heroics of the dinosaurs at the fire scene. The dinosaurs definitely had super powers beyond those of any super hero Dr. Roy had ever heard of.

"Apparently, this group of dinosaurs is called the Fossibles," Hugh Mubley continued. "They believe "anything's fossible" and they've just proven that to all of us who witnessed their heroic actions at this potentially disasterous fire."

This was the opportunity Dr. Roy had been looking for. Fame and fortune would be his if he aligned himself with the Fossibles.

With one eye still glued to the TV screen, Dr. Roy lifted the phone receiver and spoke to the hotel operator. "Please put me through to the airline. I have to get to Phoenix, Arizona as soon as I can!"

www.thefossibles.com

CHAPTER 16

Secrets Live On

That night, the Fossibles were all glad to be back in the safety and security of the Bone Zone. Earlier in the day, they feared that they'd be spending the night in jail, each in their own cell without the ability to comfort each other. Now, physically and mentally exhausted after their ordeal, they crashed into bed.

Little T fell asleep instantly and began to snore softly. Trex, on the other hand, had trouble getting to sleep. His large frame ached and seemed more unwieldy than ever as he tossed and turned within the confines of his trampoline bed. At one point, he rolled his large body over and faced the wall near his bed, the wall where the Fossilizer leaned into the corner. He plumped his pillow a couple of times and shut his eyes tightly, hoping that the self-imposed darkness would help him get to sleep. He started to count sheep, opening his left eye every now and then to sneak a peek at the bedroom wall where he visualized imaginary sheep jumping over a fence.

Still, he couldn't sleep. Finally, he rolled over on his back, eyes wide open, and stared at the ceiling. Suddenly, a red strobe-like light began pulsating in his room. He looked over and saw that the Fossilizer had come to life. The red crystal on top was lit up and spinning fast. Trex rubbed his eyes to make sure this wasn't all a dream. No, the Fossilizer really seemed alive. He jumped out of bed and bent down to pick it up.

As soon as Trex touched it, the Fossilizer began to speak. A dark, mysterious, authoritative male voice spoke his name through the end of the Fossilizer as if it were a microphone.

"Trex, are you there? Trex?" the voice asked.

At first, Trex thought he was hearing things. He rubbed his eyes again to see more clearly in the darkened room and stared intently at the Fossilizer in his hand.

"Are you there?" the voice repeated. This time, Trex knew he wasn't hearing things. Quietly and with his voice trembling with fear, he replied faintly, "Yes, I'm here. Who are you? Where are you?"

"I will tell you soon enough. But, I must talk with you and all of your brothers and sisters at the same time. Please, go get them now," the voice ordered.

Leaving the Fossilizer on his bed, Trex scurried off to arouse Deb, Riz, and Braun. "Hurry! Hurry! Come to my room. You're not going to believe this one!"

"Leave us alone, Trex. Is this some kind of a joke? Can't you see, we're sleeping," Riz stubbornly protested. "Go away."

"No. I can't go away. Trust me. You don't want to miss this one. Come on. Move it," Trex yelled over his shoulder as he ran in to wake Braun who was snoring so loudly his bed trembled. As he left their room, Deb and Riz sensed the urgency in Trex's voice and grudgingly obeyed his order.

When all the Fossibles were gathered in Trex's bedroom, he gently poked Little T. "Come on, Little T. Wake up. Something very important is happening right now. Wake up. You have to be a part of it."

Little T slowly opened his eyes. He was surprised to see all of his siblings crammed into his bedroom. He could tell from looking out his window that it was pitch dark outside, definitely not his regular morning wake up time. He quickly sat up in bed and waited to see what this was all about. He rubbed the sleep from his eyes and sat almost perfectly still.

Trex picked up the Fossilizer and, when he did, it spoke again. "Thank you, Trex, for getting your brothers and sisters together as I requested."

"What the heck?" Braun yelled, staring wide-eyed at the Fossilizer.

"Are you kidding me, Trex? Your magic stick talks?" asked a skeptical Riz.

"How cool is that?" Little T piped in. "A magic stick that talks!"

"I can't believe it," Deb said. "I can't believe it. Who is talking and how is he talking through that stick?"

The voice continued. "My name is Zigopholus, Dinosaur Magistrate from millions and millions of years ago."

The Fossibles looked at each other in amazement. Zigopholus continued.

"For all this time, I have been watching over the five of you. Shortly before all dinosaurs went extinct on planet Earth, it was I who was responsible for hiding your eggs. It was I who gave each of you unique superpowers, powers that could only be unleashed if you were born into the world. And, to make sure you were born into the world and thrived, I arranged for Joan and Clem Stone to find you. I knew that Joan would provide you with a phenomenal education. And Clem's genius for invention would provide you with hi-tech gadgets to help you navigate through the past, present and into the future. Why look what he did with the GEOGOGS ..."

"You mean you arranged for us to be found by Mom and Dad?" Deb interrupted.

"Yes, I did. And, just as I've been watching over you for millions and millions of years, I am here tonight to tell you that I will continue to do so into the future," Zigopholus answered.

"Yikes. This is getting spooky," Riz exclaimed. "Someone's been watching over us and we didn't know about it?"

"Not just anyone, Riz," Zigopholus replied. "It was me, Zigopholus, Dinosaur Magistrate."

"What shall we call you, sir?" Trex asked politely.

"You may call me Zigopholus."

"But why are you talking to us now, Zigopholus? Why didn't you talk to us as soon as Trex found the Fossilizer in the cave?" asked Deb.

"Because, my dear, there was no need for me to speak to you as long as you were in the exclusive care of Joan and Clem Stone. With them, I knew you would always be safe. But, now that you've been discovered and become worldwide celebrities overnight, I could wait no longer. The time had come for us to meet. That's why I'm talking to all of you tonight."

They all continued to listen to Zigopholus, still wide-eyed and amazed. "You, the Fossibles, have been put here on earth to use your superpowers to ward off evil and prevent disasters. And, while you're at it, help mankind avoid the mistakes of the past and show people on earth how powerful dinosaurs were and still can be. This last one has been my goal for millions and millions of years. It was also the goal of your dinosaur ancestors who labored to save you all from extinction by safeguarding your eggs."

"That's pretty ambitious, don't you think, Zigopholus?" Braun asked, a bit irreverently. "After all, there are only five of us. How can we accomplish all that you ask?"

"Yes, my son, you're right. There are only five of you. But, stop for a moment and think of all of the gifts you have been given that will help you accomplish your purposes here on earth. First, each of you has unique superpowers, powers that no human beings possess. And, when the five of you function as a team, there is no power on earth that can stop you. Second, your father, Clem, has provided you with various hi-tech gadgets like the GEOGOGS that help you see into the past. Third, you all have superior educations so that you can speak many languages, understand technology, decipher codes, navigate, and so much more. It will be easy for you to relate to all people everywhere. Fourth, you have those phenomenal motorcycles, each equipped with the latest in technology that enables you to efficiently move around in the world. And, lastly, you have me, a secret weapon to help you avoid problems in the future, problems that may not even be known to mankind at this time."

"Well, when you say it like that, Zigopholus, it does make sense. It just seems like a very tall order you're giving the five of us," Braun continued.

"It may be a tall order, Braun, but I know that you are all up to the challenge. And, I know because I personally knew the strength of all of your ancestors and the remarkable traits they handed down to each and every one of you."

"Tell us more, Zigopholus, please. This is very exciting!" Riz exclaimed.

"Yes, Riz, let me continue. Because your existence is now known to humans and, as celebrities, you're free to go anywhere in the world, I will continue to watch over you in your travels just as I've done secretly for millions and millions of years."

"How cool is that?" Little T piped in, still awed by the talking magic stick.

Zigopholus continued. "Because I am all-knowing and am continuously observing activities throughout the world, I will be extra eyes and ears for the five of you. Should it become necessary, I will warn you of danger lurking in your path."

"But, how, sir? How will you warn us?" Trex asked.

"I will communicate with you through the Fossilizer, a tool that humans must not know the power of or get in their possession. Do you understand?"

In unison, the Fossibles each shook their heads in silent agreement.

"I can't hear you, Fossibles. What did you say? Do you understand?" Zigopholus repeated sternly.

"We all said yes, sir," Braun replied apologetically for the group. "We just forgot to speak."

"Then, all is as it should be, Fossibles," Zigopholus said.

"But how will you warn us, sir?" Deb asked.

"I will get your attention by activating the Fossilizer but one of you dinosaurs must be holding it in order for me to talk to you, just as Trex is doing now. Remember, you must not tell humans that I'm communicating with you. It will be our secret, a dinosaur secret. Does that sound good to all of you?"

"It does," Riz replied. "Please don't worry about us, Zigopholus. We'll keep the secret."

Braun rolled his eyes as Riz spoke, suggesting that keeping secrets wasn't necessarily one of Riz's strongest traits.

"I see you rolling your eyes, Braun. What's wrong? Don't you think you'll be able to keep our secret?"

"We will all do as you ask," Braun said speaking for the group. As Braun spoke, each of the other Fossibles shook their head indicating agreement. "But what about telling our parents? Can we tell them?" he asked.

"Your parents have felt a special spirit surrounding them many times in the past. They just couldn't put their finger on what it was. Now, they might like to know who was behind it all and who kept moving them along on their very special journey to bring you, the Fossibles, into the world. But they too must keep the secret if you chose to tell them. OK?

"OK," Braun continued, again speaking for the group.

"Well, I have one other thing to tell you. It's about the way you've each lived your lives so far and how you must continue to live life. I know that Joan and Clem taught you sound values and that you're each a very good dinosaur. I've thought about it a lot, actually, and composed a Fossibles oath that says it all. I'd like you each to learn it so that it will help you stay grounded throughout your travels. And, just to make sure it reflects your own thoughts too, I even included one of Braun's favorite expressions."

"You did?" Braun asked, delighted by the compliment.

"I did."

"OK. Let's hear the Fossibles oath. Let it rip," Trex interjected.

"Sssh. Sssh, Trex. Show more respect," Deb whispered, holding her index finger near her mouth.

"It's OK, Deb," Zigopholus said. "I know Trex meant no disrespect. The Fossibles oath is:

I promise to respect myself, respect others, do good deeds, have integrity, and relish my ride through life because I'm BONE-A-FIDE!"

"Oh boy, BONE-A-FIDE, my favorite expression," Deb teased laughingly. "Guess I'll have to live with it from now on, right Zigopholus?"

"Right, Deb," Zigopholus said.

"OK."

"Then, for the time being, everything is as it should be. Now, get some rest. I witnessed first hand what happened to all of you today and knew that you were very frightened. I also knew that a fire was going to break out in that building so I made sure you were nearby in the police truck when it did. That way, you each had a chance to show off your super-powers and your inherent goodness. Thankfully, your deeds did not go unnoticed."

"You knew that the fire was going to break out?" Riz asked.

"Yes, I did, Riz. Didn't I tell you that I can see things in the future? After all these years of waiting, it was important that you were discovered. It was time for the entire world to learn of your existence. And, what better day than today? You are now beginning a whole new chapter in your young lives."

And, then speaking in a more serious, authoritative voice, Zigopholus signed off. "Goodnight, Fossibles, and until we speak again, say to all of us, our secret is safe. Goodnight and thank you," Zigopholus said and signed off.

Static emanated from the Fossilizer and then it went totally silent and dark. The Fossibles stared at each other and repeated in quiet unison, "Until we speak again, say to all of us, our secret is safe."

Slowly, as if in a trance, each Fossible returned to their bedroom and crawled under the covers. This time, a quiet peace instantly engulfed each of them and they quickly fell into a deep, deep sleep.

www.thefossibles.com

CHAPTER 17

Rock Stars

While Zigopholus was secretly visiting in the Bone Zone, Joan was busy handling numerous requests for personal appearances by the Fossibles. Her phone was ringing off the hook. The President of the United States, the Governor of Arizona, a paleontologist in Hawaii, and several others called. Joan couldn't believe all the important people she talked to that night. Just 24 hours earlier, there was no way that Joan or Clem could have contemplated such a dramatic change in their family. They continued to hope and pray for only the best for their five children.

Later that same evening, a gigantic mustard yellow SUV drove up the Stones' long driveway spewing clouds of brownish red dust into the hot night air. Suddenly, the driver's side door opened and out jumped an odd-looking, tanned man wearing a dark vest, dungarees, high boots, and a crisply starched white button shirt. He gingerly leapt up onto the porch and knocked ferociously on the front door. Joan opened it and the stranger thrust out his hand, introducing himself as Dr. Dimitri Roy, a world famous paleontologist. Simultaneously, he handed Joan one of his business cards, stained and a bit tattered on the edges.

"Please, come inside," Joan said, ushering him into the living room. "Clem, there's a Dr. Roy here. He wants to talk to us."

Clem came into the room and stopped dead in his tracks.

"Hello, Dr. Roy. Nice to see you again," he said as he stepped closer and extended his hand to shake.

"Same here." The two men shook hands.

"I don't understand, Clem. Do you two know each other?"

"Yes. A few months ago, I fixed Dr. Roy's SUV for him. Remember the big mustard yellow SUV that surprised us one day when all the kids ran back to the Bone Zone?"

"Oh, yes."

"Ah, the Bone Zone. So that's what you call that big building out back, huh? I wondered about how there could be enough folks in this neck of the woods to warrant big events like you told me."

"I had to tell you something to protect the Fossibles."

"I understand."

Then, Dr. Roy continued, "Mr. and Mrs. Stone, once I heard about your dinosaurs, I flew right to Phoenix from a conference I was attending in London. I have come here at this late hour to personally congratulate you on how well you've raised the Fossibles. As you both know, within the scientific community there is already intense interest in the Fossibles. News spread quickly among all the conference attendees as we awoke in the middle of the night to watch live footage of the fire on TV. I suspect that interest will only become more and more intense as each day goes by. Based on my knowledge, experience, and notoriety in the scientific community, I can be a great asset to you in caring for the Fossibles."

"Go on, Dr. Roy, tell us more. How can you help us?" Clem prodded.

"I want to offer you my personal services as the Fossibles' guardian whenever they travel the world for scientific research purposes. With my connections and the respect I command among my peers, I'll make sure that their care is always the best it can be, no compromises, I promise," Dr. Roy responded, letting his voice trail off as he waited for Joan or Clem to reply.

"OK. What do you need to know to get started?"

"First, when were they born?"

Just as Dr. Roy was introducing himself to Joan and Clem, the Fossilizer came alive again in Trex's bedroom out in the Bone Zone. The red crystal flashed wildly and spun frantically. Highly agitated, it was signaling for someone to pick it up.

But, Trex and Little T were sound asleep, too asleep to notice. After all, it had been a very long, very hard day.

And, in their sleep, the Fossibles heard the following phrase repeating itself inside their heads: "Until we speak again, say to all of us, our secret is safe."

— To Be Continued —

Photo Album

Joan and Clem Stone

The Fossibles ...

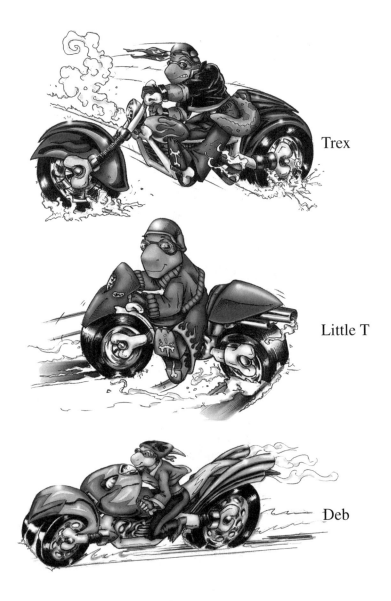

Trex

Little T

Deb

... *Love to Ride*

Riz

Braun

Dr. Dimitri Roy

The Bone Zone

www.thefossibles.com